T0173096

Smart Card Security

Smart Card Security
Applications, Attacks, and Countermeasures

B.B. Gupta
Megha Quamara

CRC Press
Taylor & Francis Group
Boca Raton London New York

CRC Press is an imprint of the
Taylor & Francis Group, an **informa** business

CRC Press
Taylor & Francis Group
6000 Broken Sound Parkway NW, Suite 300
Boca Raton, FL 33487-2742

© 2020 by Taylor & Francis Group, LLC
CRC Press is an imprint of Taylor & Francis Group, an Informa business

No claim to original U.S. Government works

Printed on acid-free paper

International Standard Book Number-13: 978-0-367-35440-4 (Hardback)

Visit the Taylor & Francis Web site at
http://www.taylorandfrancis.com

and the CRC Press Web site at
http://www.crcpress.com

Dedicated to my parents and family for their constant support during the course of this book.

—*B. B. Gupta*

Dedicated to my mentor, my parents, and my friends for their constant encouragement and belief during the course of this book.

—*Megha Quamara*

Contents

Figures

Tables

Preface

Smart card technology has outperformed other conventional technologies as a result of its superior capabilities. Rapid advancement in the technology has led to an all-time high demand for smart cards. They provide enormous benefits to business and computing systems with their portability and secure data storage capability. Smart cards are resistant to various attacks due to their self-containment property, which reduces their dependability on external resources that are vulnerable to security threats. Hence, they are a popular choice for transactions and identification among various applications, including authentication, single sign on (SSO), and so forth. However, malicious attackers are always looking for ways to bypass the security mechanisms. Confidentiality and integrity of the data stored or transmitted by smart card systems are always at stake. This requires constant improvement in the technology with respect to security at various levels or related to various components. Proper analysis, deployment, testing, and auditing of security measures should be ensured. This book provides a broad overview of smart card technology and its various applications. It familiarizes readers with the security attacks associated with smart card–based systems and applications, along with their appropriate countermeasures.

Specifically, the chapters contained in this book are summarized as follows:

Chapter 1: Smart Cards: Evolution, Statistics, and Forecasts

This chapter introduces the concept of smart cards as a starting point for the newcomers in the field. It illuminates the past events associated with the evolution of smart cards, along with some related statistics and industrial forecasts provided by some of the well-known organizations across the world, in order to showcase the growing usage trends of this technology.

Chapter 2: Classification of Smart Cards and How They Work

This chapter discusses different types of smart cards that are in use today, including various aspects regarding their configuration, underlying operating system, usage, and so forth. It also discusses in detail how a typical smart card–based system works, including the different entities involved and how transmission of information among them takes place using application protocol data units (APDUs).

Chapter 3: Hardware-Level Security Attacks and Logical Threats in Smart Cards

This chapter discusses different hardware- and software-level security attacks in smart card–based systems and applications and the appropriate countermeasures for these security attacks.

Chapter 4: Data Security in Smart Cards

This chapter discusses the security attacks on confidentiality, integrity, and availability of data in smart card–based systems and applications, including unauthorized remote monitoring, communication protocol exploitation, denial of service (DoS) attacks, and so forth, and presents the possible countermeasures for these attacks.

Chapter 5: Remote User Authentication Mechanisms in Smart Card–Based Applications

This chapter discusses security attacks against remote user authentication mechanisms in smart card–based applications and proposes a possible countermeasure for these attacks. The focus of this chapter is on the security of key management techniques, hash functions, cryptographic techniques, digital certificates, and signatures.

Chapter 6: Smart Card Communication Standards, Applications, and Development Tools

This chapter covers different communication standards for smart card–based applications and discusses the role of smart cards in various application areas. It also discusses various open-source tools for the development and maintenance of smart card–based systems and applications.

Chapter 7: Blockchain Integration and Quantum Smart Cards

This chapter focuses on the role of blockchain technology for securing smart card–based transactions and quantum cryptography for designing secure smart card–based algorithms.

Acknowledgment

Many people have contributed greatly to this book, *Smart Card Security: Applications, Attacks, and Countermeasures*. The authors would like to acknowledge all of them for their valuable help and generous ideas in improving the quality of this book. With our feelings of gratitude, we would like to introduce them in turn. First, we thank the CRC Press/Taylor and Francis Group staff, especially Richard O'Hanley and his team, for their constant encouragement, continuous assistance, and untiring support. Without their technical support, this book would not be completed. We also thank our families for being a source of continuous love, unconditional support, and prayers not only for this work, but throughout our life. Last but far from least, we express our heartfelt thanks to the Almighty for bestowing over us the courage to face the complexities of life and to complete this work.

May 2019
B. B. Gupta
Megha Quamara

About the Authors

B. B. Gupta received his PhD from the Indian Institute of Technology, Roorkee, India, in the area of Information and Cyber Security. He has published more than 200 research papers in international journals and conferences of high repute, including IEEE, Elsevier, ACM, Springer, Wiley, Taylor & Francis, and Inderscience. He has visited several countries, including Canada, Japan, Malaysia, Australia, China, Hong Kong, Italy, and Spain, to present his research work. His biography was selected and published in the 30th edition of *Marquis Who's Who in the World*, 2012. Dr. Gupta also received a Young Faculty research fellowship award from the Ministry of Electronics and Information Technology, Government of India, in 2018. He is also working as principal investigator of various R&D projects. He is serving as associate editor of IEEE Access and IEEE TII and executive editor of IJITCA and Inderscience. At present, Dr. Gupta is working as assistant professor in the Department of Computer Engineering, National Institute of Technology, Kurukshetra, India. His research interests include information security, cyber security, mobile security, cloud computing, web security, intrusion detection, and phishing.

Megha Quamara received her Master of Technology (M.Tech.) degree specialized in cyber security from the National Institute of Technology (NIT), Kurukshetra, India, in the year 2018. She was awarded the Gold Medal for being the best graduating student throughout the course. She received her Bachelor of Technology (B.Tech.) degree in Computer Science and Engineering from the University Institute of Engineering and Technology (UIET), Kurukshetra University, India, in 2015, with a First Division with Honour. Her research interests include security in Internet of Things (IoT) and cloud computing, authentication in smart card technology, security in autonomous vehicles, and data privacy. She has published and presented nine research papers (including one book chapter)

in international journals and conferences of high repute, including Wiley, Elsevier, IEEE, and Springer. She is also serving as reviewer of various journals and conferences. Soon, she will start pursuing a doctoral degree at CEA, Paris, in collaboration with the University of Toulouse, France, where her main area of work will be safety and security of cyber-physical systems.

Smart Cards
Evolution, Statistics, and Forecasts

1

1.1 INTRODUCTION

For years, smart cards (also known as integrated circuit [IC] cards) have been used as easy-to-carry pocket-size computers for storing and processing private information of the users, along with communicating with other computing systems through wired or wireless connections [1]. These cards have a crucial role in transaction-based applications [2] and have found extensive use in wide range of such applications including user authentication (e.g., membership cards, access control cards) [3], health-care (e.g., e-health cards) [4], finance (e.g., debit or credit cards) [5], transportation (e.g., transit fare payment cards) [6], telecommunication (e.g., subscriber identity module [SIM] cards) [7], retail (loyalty cards) [8], entertainment (e.g., paid televisions) [9], smart documents (electronic passports) [10], and so forth. These enable tracking consumers' transactions, which can be interlinked with the remote database servers for predictive analysis and other such applications.

In comparison to other platforms, smart card–based applications are significantly different in terms of their development and how they work. These are characterized as self-contained, economically efficient, reliable, tamper-proof, and highly secured information systems. These have lower maintenance cost than their other counterparts, including barcodes and magnetic stripe cards [11–13]. Moreover, they support more functionality and can handle more information. Latest advancements in data assimilation, storage, processing, and transmission technologies, such as near field communication (NFC), machine-to-machine (M2M) communication, embedded programming, electron beam lithography, and so forth, are providing opportunities to the card manufacturers to add multiple functionalities on them. In addition, they provide organizations an effective tool to expand their services to the authorized individuals and prevent complex identification processes. To improve resource efficiency, smart card–based applications are deployed on multiserver architectures. Increasing security and data breaches are among some of the propelling factors for bringing them toward the forefront of business-related transactions. Smart card technology encompasses essential components required for exchanging data across any kind of network.

Apart from the previously discussed benefits, smart cards also possess certain limitations, including limited computing capabilities and storage, and are often dependent on smart card readers for clock and power mechanism. Various security- and privacy-related issues are also a matter of concern. Issues of their coexistence with already established technologies along with the global acceptance of technological standards associated with smart cards need to be addressed. Moreover, understanding of the long-term benefits of the technology is needed.

Before going into the details of smart card technology, evolutionary aspects are considered first in the next section.

1.2 EVOLUTION OF SMART CARDS

With their advent, smart cards benefited businesses in their evolution and the expansion of their services and products in the changing and competitive global marketplace. To understand the future scope of operation of smart cards, it is necessary to consider their historical development and the influence of other technologies on them. A number of milestones were achieved in the development and adoption of smart card technology, as summarized in Table 1.1.

The concept of the smart card came into being in the early 1970s through research and development in some of the most technologically innovative nations across the world, including Germany, France, and Japan [14]. Apart from independent research, major commercial manufacturers across the globe started collaborating with each other to make enhancements in smart card technology. Initial efforts were made to replace hard cash with e-cash in remote payment-based applications to reduce the cash-handling cost and to ensure security against theft risks. Later on, smart cards found their use

TABLE 1.1 Major historical events associated with smart card technology

YEAR	EVENT
1968–1969	First patent to realize the idea of plastic cards with embedded microchips or automated chip cards was filed by two German engineers, inventors, and associates—Jürgen Dethloff and Helmut Grötrupp.
1970	First and only patent on the idea of smart card was filed in Japan by Dr. Kunitaka Arimura.
1974	Patent for integrated chip (IC) card, later named as smart card, was filed by French engineer and inventor Roland Moreno.
1975	Roland Moreno received first smart card patent in France.
1976	Patent on memory and microcontroller-based smart cards was filed by Jürgen Dethloff.
1977	Three French commercial manufacturers—Bull CP8, Schlumberger, and SGS Thomson—became involved in development of IC cards.
1978	Roland Moreno received smart card patent in United States; Michel Ugon filed a patent for a self-programmable one-chip microcomputer (SPOM).
1979	First secure and single-chip microprocessor-based smart card for French banking industry was developed by Motorola.
1980	Smart cards underwent first mass test in three French cities.
1982	United States led its first smart card trial in New Jersey and North Dakota.
1983	Charles Walton, an inventor, was granted with a patent associated with radiofrequency identification (RFID).
1985	Bull CP8 launched first banking card with embedded microcontroller.
1986	Clients associated with Bank of Virginia and Maryland were provided with cards equipped with Bull CP8.
1987	U.S. Department of Agriculture adopted Peanut Marketing Card.
1992	Magnetic stripe cards in French financial institutions were replaced with Carte Bleue debit cards. Patent filed by Jürgen Dethloff and Helmut Grötrupp was registered and approved by the authorities.
1993	Europay, MasterCard, and Visa (EMV) global technical standard for smart payment cards was written.
1994	Release of first version of EMV system; ISO/IEC 14443 standard's development was assigned to Working Group 8 of Subcommittee 17 (SC 17/WG 8).
1995	Around 3,000,000 mobile phone subscribers across the globe started paying bills using smart cards.

(Continued)

TABLE 1.1 *(Continued)* Major historical events associated with smart card technology

YEAR	EVENT
1996	VISA launched cash cards in Olympic Games at Atlanta.
1997	Launch of multiapplication operating system (MULTOS).*
1998	Smart cards entered French healthcare system. Development of first prototype of Java Card Open Platform (JC/OP). Windows-based smart card operating system was announced by Microsoft.
1999	GlobalPlatform, a nonprofit organization that creates and publishes secure chip technology specifications, was founded. Finland launched national eID cards.
2001	U.S. Department of Defense issued Military Common Access Card (CAC) credentials for physical (access control) and logical security (authentication). GlobalPlatform Card Specification v2.1 was published.
2003	Near field communication (NFC) was approved as an ISO/IEC and ECMA standard.
2003–2005	Dot Net Cards under development.
2004	Version of contactless cards by VISA and MasterCard was deployed in United States.
2005	First acceptance of EMV-compliant cards in Malaysia and International Civil Aviation Organization (ICAO)–compliant electronic passports in Norway.
2006	Gemalto was founded by collaboration of world's top two smart card manufacturers at that time, Axalto and Gemplus. Department of Defense published a document entitled "Implementation Guide for CAC Next Generation (NG)" defining guidelines for the implementation of government's Federal Information Processing Standard 201 (FIPS 201) Personal Identity Verification (PIV).
2007	Smart Payment Association (SPA)** conducted an internal market monitoring that showed inclination of financial institutions toward smart card security.
2008	Public key infrastructure (PKI)–based smart card management systems were deployed for the first time on a large scale. Next-generation Java Card 3.0 was launched.
2009	Japan manufactured reusable smart cards for financial applications.
2014	MasterCard became the first company to accept EMV cards in United States; 3.4 billion EMV card holders worldwide.
2015	Global smart card market was dominated by Asia-Pacific smart card market.

(Continued)

TABLE 1.1 *(Continued)* Major historical events associated with smart card technology

YEAR	EVENT
2016	6.07 billion EMV card holders across the globe, as reported by member financial institutions of JCB, American Express, Visa, MasterCard, UnionPay, and Discover.
2017	Payment Summit by International Card Manufacturing Association (ICMA) and Smart Card Alliance.***
2018	Eurosmart predicted global smart card market to exceed 3 billion in terms of number of units distributed.

*MULTOS is an open standard under the control of MULTOS Consortium, which allows support to multiple applications on the same smart card chip [15].

**SPA is a nonprofit organization that provides secure payment technology across the world by addressing the current issues associated with the growing payment environment [16].

***Smart Card Alliance (also known as Secure Technology Alliance) is a nonprofit association that works on embedded chip technology for the widespread adoption of smart cards [17].

in various application areas including telecommunications, defense, public transport, and so forth. Multiapplication smart cards, with their enormous potential, significantly changed the market of smart cards and their associated industries.

1.3 RELATED STATISTICS

EMVCo stated that there were approximately 7.0 billion EMV card holders by the end of 2017, and of all the global card-based transactions, 63.7% used EMV chip technology [18]. Figure 1.1 shows the percentage of EMV-based card-present transactions across the world for the period from June 2017 to July 2018 [19]. Figure 1.2 shows the EMV chip card adoption rate across the globe for 3 consecutive years (i.e., from 2015 to 2017) [19].

With increasing use of smart cards for transactions, various applications and services also faced financial losses due to card fraud across the globe. Figure 1.3 depicts that the financial losses due to card fraud across the globe increased by nearly four-fold over an 8-year span from 2010 to 2018 [20]. In 2017, approximately 200,000 Visa and MasterCard credit card accounts were stolen by Equifax hackers in United States by exploiting the storage tables that contained transactional history of the customers [21].

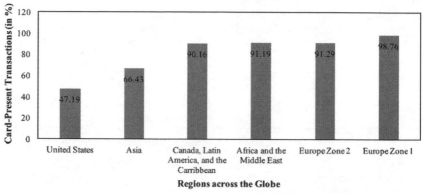

FIGURE 1.1   Global smart card market trends and forecasts (2018).

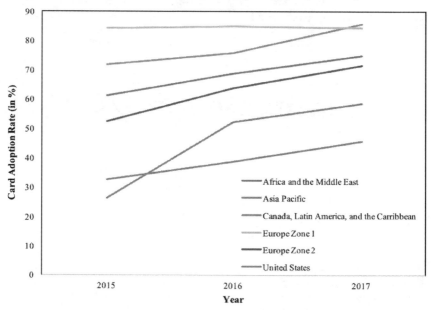

FIGURE 1.2   EMV chip card adoption rate.

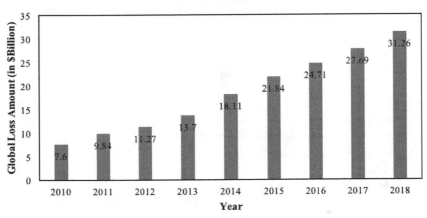

FIGURE 1.3 Financial losses due to global card fraud.

Eurosmart provided the statistics and forecasts associated with the shipment of secure elements for smart cards in five areas, including telecommunications, banking and finance, government, device manufacturers, and others (e.g., transport, paid television, and access control) from the year 2010 to 2018, as shown in Table 1.2 [22].

TABLE 1.2 Secure element shipment (in millions) statistics (2010–2018)

	APPLICATION AREA				
YEAR	TELECOM-MUNICA-TIONS	BANKING AND FINANCE	GOVERN-MENT	DEVICE MANUFACTURERS	OTHERS
2010	4,200	880	190	—	250
2011	4,700	1,050	240	-	305
2012	5,100	1,200	310	-	360
2013	4,850	1,550	350	-	390
2014	5,200	2,050	380	190	420
2015	5,300	2,850	410	310	450
2016	5,450	2,900	460	330	470
2017	5,600	3,000	485	400	190
2018	5,600	3,150	510	470	185

1.4 INDUSTRIAL FORECASTS

Technavio, a leading advisory and research company, conducted a comprehensive market study, according to which the compound annual growth rate (CAGR) for the contactless smart card market for the banking sector across the globe is expected to reach about 33% by 2025, and a growth of more than 8% is expected in CAGR for the smart card IC market from 2016 to 2020 [23]. Smart card device manufacturing is predicted to be the fastest-growing segment, with an expected growth rate of 19% during the 4-year span from 2016 to 2020.

According to Persistence Market Research, the IC market will hold approximately 84.9% of the market share in the year 2026 [24]. Global smart cards market revenue is expected to reach $20 thousand million by the year 2026. The government sector, in terms of consumption of smart cards, will reach 773 million units by the year 2024.

According to a Nilson Report published in 2017, the purchase amount of services and goods using cards from the brand JCB, American Express, VISA, Discover/Diners Club, and MasterCard will reach $54.891 trillion by 2025 [20]. In addition, these cards will be a part of 767 billion such transactions [25]. The projected global card fraud cost for the year 2025 is expected to be $50 billion [26].

According to *Forbes*, financial losses due to card fraud in the United States is expected to exceed $12 billion by the year 2020 [27]. According to Eurosmart, the global market for smart cards will cross 10 billion in terms of number of units, which means that the trend in overall growth will be close to 3% for 2018 [12].

1.5 CONCLUSION

With already existing and predictable benefits, smart card technology is seeking attention of both public and private sectors across the globe, as it provides various stakeholders with an indispensable tool to assimilate services and products in real time. This chapter provided a brief introduction to smart card technology and highlighted the past events associated with the development of smart cards and related aspects. Some of the industrial statistics and forecasts associated with the domain were also discussed.

In the next chapter, we will investigate the taxonomy of smart cards and will present details regarding how a typical smart card–based system and application works.

REFERENCES

1. Vanderhoof, R., & Smart Card Alliance. (2017). Smart card talk. Retrieved from https://www.securetechalliance.org/wp-content/uploads/smartcardtalk-2017Q1.pdf

2. Mayes, K. E., & Markantonakis, K. (2008). *Smart cards, tokens, security and applications* (Vol. 1). New York, NHY: Springer.

3. Jones, L. A., Antón, A. I., & Earp, J. B. (2007, October). Towards understanding user perceptions of authentication technologies. In *Proceedings of the 2007 ACM workshop on Privacy in electronic society* (pp. 91–98). ACM. Retrieved from https://dl.acm.org/citation.cfm?id=1314352

4. Andreassen, H. K., Bujnowska-Fedak, M. M., Chronaki, C. E., Dumitru, R. C., Pudule, I., Santana, S., ... & Wynn, R. (2007). European citizens' use of E-health services: a study of seven countries. *BMC Public Health*, 7(1), 53.

5. Nadarajan, S. (2017). A comparative study of financial transaction cards: Credit & debit cards. Retrieved from http://ijsrcseit.com/paper/CSEIT1726181.pdf

6. Dixon, P. B., Cook, T., Mistry, P., & Koenig, J. (2018). U.S. Patent No. 9,996,985. Washington, DC: U.S. Patent and Trademark Office.

7. Howard, P. (2016). U.S. Patent No. 9,357,375. Washington, DC: U.S. Patent and Trademark Office.

8. Aloni, R. L., Axelrod, B. T., Bowman, J. L., Funda, J. J., Polon, J. S., & Tiku, S. V. (2016). U.S. Patent No. 9,430,773. Washington, DC: U.S. Patent and Trademark Office.

9. Lindholm, R. A. (2017). U.S. Patent No. 9,686,632. Washington, DC: U.S. Patent and Trademark Office.

10. Maitra, S. (2018). A brief study of smart card based electronic passport, resident identity card and driving license projects in India. *International Journal of Engineering Technology Science and Research*, 5(4), 89–96.

11. Martin, D. A., Dean, S. A., Waechter, M. L., & Winters, G. P. (2016). U.S. Patent No. 9,290,338. Washington, DC: U.S. Patent and Trademark Office.

12. Nedjah, N., Wyant, R. S., Mourelle, L. M., & Gupta, B. B. (2019). Efficient fingerprint matching on smart cards for high security and privacy in smart systems. *Information Sciences*, 479, 622–639.

13. Nedjah, N., Wyant, R. S., Mourelle, L. M., & Gupta, B. B. (2017). Efficient yet robust biometric iris matching on smart cards for data high security and privacy. *Future Generation Computer Systems*, 76, 18–32. Retrieved from https://www.gemalto.com/companyinfo/smart-cards-basics

14. Shelfer, K. M., & Procaccino, J. D. (2002). Smart card evolution. *Communications of the ACM*, 45(7), 83–88.

15. Elliott, J. (1999). The one-card trick. Multi-application smart card E-commerce prototypes. *Computing & Control Engineering Journal*, 10(3), 121–128.

16. Smart Payment Association. (n.d.). Homepage. Retrieved from http://www.smartpaymentassociation.com

17. Smart Card Alliance. (n.d.). Homepage. Retrieved from http://www.smartcardalliance.org

18. Secure Technology Alliance. (n.d.). Financial applications. https://www.securetechalliance.org/smart-cards-applications-financial/
19. EMVCo. (2018). Deployment statistics. Retrieved from https://www.emvco.com/about/deployment-statistics/
20. The Nilson Report. (2019). Charts and graphs archive. Retrieved from https://www.nilsonreport.com/publication_chart_and_graphs_archive.php
21. Krebson Security. (2017). Equifax Hackers Stole 200k Credit Card Accounts in One Fell Swoop. Retrieved from https://krebsonsecurity.com/2017/09/equifax-hackers-stole-200k-credit-card-accounts-in-one-fell-swoop/#more-40773
22. Eurosmart. (2018). Secure elements shipments from 2010 to 2018. Retrieved from https://www.eurosmart.com/facts-and-figures/
23. Technavio. (2016). Global contactless smart cards market 2016-2020. Retrieved from https://www.technavio.com/report/global-automatic-identification-system-contactless-smartcards-market
24. Perdistence Market Research. (2018). Global market study on smart cards: North America to remain dominant regional market through 2026. Retrieved from https://www.persistencemarketresearch.com/market-research/smart-cards-market.asp
25. The Nilson Report. (2018). Charts & graphs archive, 2018. Retrieved from https://nilsonreport.com/publication_chart_and_graphs_archive.php?1=1&year=2018
26. The Nilson Report. (2018). Global card fraud to reach $43.8B; Visa claims resolution (VCR) to help merchants, with caveat. Retrieved from https://nilsonreport.com/upload/pdf/Global_Card_Fraud_to_Reach_43.8B_Visa_.pdf
27. Forbes. U.S. card fraud losses could exceed $12B by 2020. Retrieved from https://www.forbes.com/sites/rogeraitken/2016/10/26/us-card-fraud-losses-could-exceed-12bn-by-2020/#2f073c66d243

Classification of Smart Cards and How They Work

2

2.1 INTRODUCTION

Smart cards can be distinguished based on the kind of chip embedded in them, how data are read or written from or to the chip, nature of hardware architecture, electrical characteristics of the circuit, shape, size, cost, capabilities, security features, and card services. Different application types have different requirements associated with memory sizes and processor logic for performing complex tasks. Choosing a specific technology depends on these requirements and factors, including class of application, financial aspects of the business model, security requirements, hardware and software platform availability, cost, and so forth. In the next section, a detailed taxonomy of smart cards is provided, and various aspects related to smart cards are discussed.

2.2 CLASSIFICATION OF SMART CARDS

Figure 2.1 depicts various types of smart cards categorized based on capabilities/configuration, security features, communication interface or connection to smart card reader, type of embedded components, nature of real-time

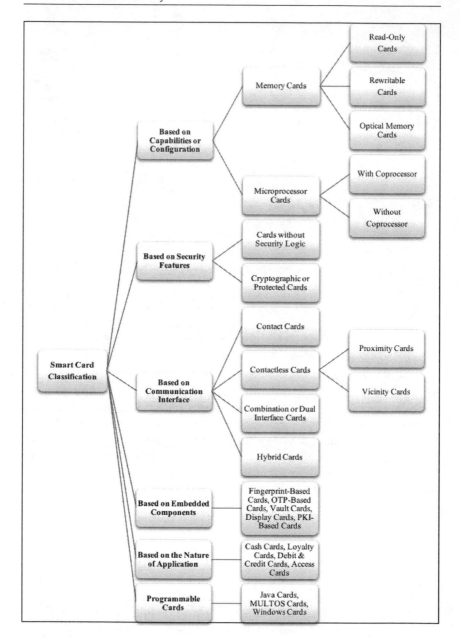

FIGURE 2.1   Smart cards classification.

applications, and type of operating system used [1]. These categories and their different subtypes are discussed in the following subsections.

2.2.1 Based on Capabilities or Configuration

Following are the types of smart cards based on capabilities or configuration:

1. **Memory cards**—These cards are installed with a memory chip with no processing capabilities. Data are read from and can be written once to the initialized fixed address locations on the chip in different ways [2]. Read-only memory cards, also known as straight memory cards, store information that cannot be manipulated. Thus, they have limited functionality and lower cost [3]. The commands and the instructions are burned into the memory. These cards lack lock mechanisms or security logic and are identified by the host system on insertion into the card reader. These cards can be easily duplicated and cannot be tracked by the identifier present over the card and, thus, are known as straight memory cards [4]. These are typically used for identification tasks and as prepaid phone cards that are discarded once the already stored credit value runs out. Rewritable cards, on the other hand, are reusable and contain certain logic that provides controlled access to the memory locations and capability of adding, updating, or deleting the data stored on them through a secure key mechanism [5]. These cards can also be impersonated by attackers and can be tracked by on-card identifiers. Optical memory cards use laser-sensitive optical storage medium for storing information [6]. They provide a durable platform for carrying security-intensive and tamper-proof data that can be either text or image. A rectilinear format is used in these cards in which tracks are in the form of arrays. These cards are typically used in biometrics-based applications.
2. **Microprocessor cards**—These cards contain a specialized microprocessor chip embedded within the card that enables multiple tasks, including memory allocation and file access, and also provide on-card data processing capabilities [7]. A software called Card Operating System (COS) enables microprocessor chips to organize data and information into file structures and provides controlled access to user memory (usually electrically erasable

programmable read only memory [EEPROM]) present on the card [8]. These cards support dynamic software updating without requiring any hardware changes and support multiple functionalities. However, limited memory and processing capability limits the performance of these cards. Microprocessor cards with embedded coprocessors provide improved flexibility and enhanced level of processing and encryption speed.

2.2.2 Based on Security Features

Some smart cards are unprotected in the sense that they do not support any security mechanism. However, there are cards that use secure system keys or passwords with encryption mechanisms to provide secure identification, and these are known as protected or cryptographic smart cards [9]. These cards have certain built-in logic that ensures controlled access to the card memory or can be configured in a manner to enable read and write protect. These cards cannot be duplicated and can be tracked by an on-card identifier. These are typically used in single sign-on (SSO)–based applications, banking, subscriber identity module (SIM), e-passports, and so forth. The algorithms supported by these cards typically include symmetric cryptography (e.g., Advanced Encryption Standard [AES], Data Encryption Standard [DES], triple DES), asymmetric cryptography (e.g., Rivest-Shamir-Adleman [RSA], Diffie-Hellman key exchange, elliptic curve cryptography [ECC]), random number generation, message digest (e.g., Message Digest (MD5), Secure Hash Algorithm (SHA), Keyed-Hash Message Authentication Code (HMAC)), and so forth [10]. Microprocessor-based smart cards with coprocessors supporting cryptographic algorithms are known as crypto-coprocessors [11].

2.2.3 Based on Communication Interface

Smart cards can be classified into four types based on communication interface, as follows:

1. **Contact cards**—Contact cards work by coming in physical contact with the reader to transmit the information [12]. On insertion of the card inside the reader, the gold-plated electrical contacts present over the card surface come in contact with the reader, and on establishment of the contact, data, commands, and card status are transmitted to the reader for further processing and storage. These

cards obtain power for functioning from the reader. They are used in various applications including telecommunication (SIM cards in mobile phones), banking, electronic purse, and so forth.

2. **Contactless cards**—These cards do not require any physical contact with the reader and can transfer data to the reader through radiofrequency identification (RFID) or electromagnetic radiation using an antenna present on both the card and the reader [13]. Cards that are not self-powered when they come in proximity of the reader obtain power through the electromagnetic field. Contactless cards come in two varieties: proximity and vicinity cards. Proximity cards are either memory or microprocessor based and have a communication range of a few centimeters. These are read-only cards with limited memory and are commonly used for identification purposes for secure access to buildings. Vicinity cards, on the other hand, have a communication range of up to a meter and can also be either memory or microprocessor based. Drawbacks of contactless smart cards include restrictions on distance from the reader, compatibility issues, limited use of cryptographic mechanisms, limited user memory, and higher costs.

3. **Combination or dual-interface cards**—In combination or dual-interface cards, a single chip supports and controls interfaces that are used to serve the purpose of both contact and contactless communication through either contact pads or embedded antenna and, hence, are capable of supporting multiple applications [14]. These cards are commonly used in a variety of applications including government applications and banking due to the ease of use and enhanced security they provide.

4. **Hybrid cards**—Hybrid cards are similar to combination cards in the sense that they also support interfaces for both contact and contactless communication installed on the same card [15]. However, separate and isolated chips are installed on them for each interface that are not connected to each other (e.g., a microprocessor contact interface chip, along with a proximity or contactless RFID chip). The contact chip is typically significant for applications demanding high levels of security, whereas the contactless chip is appropriate for fast transactions. The processors associated with these chips cannot be updated at the same time. Example applications involving the use of hybrid cards include the following: a card supporting remote cash transactions using a contactless interface and recharging using a contact interface and identification cards supporting network access through a contact chip and attendance marking using a proximity chip.

2.2.4 Based on Embedded Components

Smart cards, apart from a standard chip, can also contain more embedded electronic components that are specific for certain business solutions. These are also known as multicomponent cards and can be considered as an outcome of technological innovation. For example, cards may contain a fingerprint sensor present on the card surface that is used for user identification and verification [16]. The fingerprints of the users are stored securely on the card and are tamper-proof. Encryption, decryption, and verification processes occur on the card itself and do not require transmission of information to the remote server. One-time password (OTP)–based cards are typically used in net-banking and e-commerce applications. These cards involve generation of an OTP, which is displayed on an online application associated with them for verification [17]. Vault cards contain rewritable magnetic stripes. To activate these cards, the user has to enter a personal identification number (PIN) value on the card. Upon successful verification of the PIN, the merchant module on the card becomes activated and transactions can be made [18]. This process is repeated for other transactions as well. These cards are highly secure in the sense that the PIN value is not delivered through the network. Display cards use a light-emitting diode (LED) or liquid crystal display (LCD) screen on the card to display information [19]. They may also come with touch-sensitive buttons that enable enhanced control and security features. Some multicomponent smart cards may also come with an on-card battery, which enables local processing on the card without any dependency on the readers for the battery power. These are also known as self-powered cards. Public key infrastructure (PKI)–based cards contain a digital certificate issued by a PKI provider that is stored in the card with some additional information for authentication purposes [20]. Use of multicomponent cards is expected to grow at a fast pace because of some of their advantages, including improved information security, enhanced processing speed, ease of use, and other facilities.

2.2.5 Based on the Nature of Application

Application-specific cards work for single type of application. Cash cards, also known as data cards, store cash value, which is loaded by a particular retail store, and after the purchase, the card's value is updated by subtracting the amount spent in purchase from the stored value [21]. These promote cashless transactions that are typically involved in buying goods and services. To provide benefits to their customers, retailers issue loyalty cards that contain discount-related information, credit amount, and other information and are used to obtain transactional benefits. Finance cards include debit and credit cards [22]. Debit cards contains value that is associated with the amount of money stored in a user's bank account, which can be used to make transactions. Credit cards allow card holders to borrow money from the issuer of the card to make purchases. Access control cards ensure that only identified users can access the restricted areas or buildings and physical assets in an organization [23].

Multiapplication smart cards are also becoming popular these days and can support various applications on a single card [24]. These applications reside on separate memory segments, and memory allocation of application-specific data along with data retrieval is handled by the microprocessor present on the card. For example, Blue from American Express supports two applications, including online banking, in which it ensures extra security, and a ticketing application, in which it verifies the ticket order of the card holder [25].

2.2.6 Programmable Cards

Programmable cards contain a dynamic application card operating system that enables separate memory allocation for the operating system and application, which causes easy card updating. Examples of programmable cards include Java Cards, multiapplication operating system (MULTOS) cards, and Windows-based cards. These allow third parties to load, update, and delete the application logic dynamically on the smart card chip, thereby supporting multiple applications on the same chip. The operating system and the applications are allocated with separate memory, thus making it easier to update the card regardless of the data stored on the card.

Java Card platform was developed by Sun Microsystems and is managed by Oracle. In these cards, Java-based applications are made to run over the smart card chip, and these applications can be ported to different smart cards using a virtual machine and runtime library. These cards are typically used in highly security-intensive applications including telecommunications and finance [26].

MULTOS stands for multiapplication operating system, and these cards can support multiple applications. These were initially designed for providing efficient security procedures for managing security-intensive real-time applications [27]. They allow application loading and deletion at any point when the card is active. Unlike Java Cards, these require a specific or already defined mechanism to load applications on the card chip. Application loading involves transmission of the application code as well as the certificate to the chip, which can be deleted at any point in time. Each application's code and data are stored at a separate memory location, and an application cannot directly access another application's logical area or memory space, which when attempted, leads to process abortion. MULTOS cards typically use public-key cryptographic mechanisms, including digital certificates, instead of symmetric key sharing. MULTOS cards are used for many applications, including finance, authentication, loyalty, e-identity, and military access control.

Smart cards compatible with Microsoft's Windows operating system also exist and can support various Microsoft-compatible security applications, including virtual private network (VPN), secure web access, Windows domain log-on, Outlook sign in and encryption, and so forth [28]. These smart cards are available as contact, contactless, and dual-interface cards.

2.3 HOW SMART CARD–BASED SYSTEMS WORK

A smart card is constructed using plastic and contains an embedded computer chip. This chip can be either a microprocessor (microcontroller) chip, which can process the incoming or stored data, or a memory chip, which can store the raw or processed data [1, 23]. The chip typically has a layered architecture that consists of integrated layers of different materials (e.g., polyvinyl chloride [PVC] or polycarbonate) with high durability and specific functionality. The data correspond to some value used for transactional purposes or some information that can be used for identification. The microprocessor chip or a smart card reader performs transactions over the data. The reader is either in direct contact with the smart card or indirectly in contact via electromagnetic or radiofrequency communication. This communication involves use of synchronous protocols accompanied by the transmission of application protocol data units (APDUs), which are small-size data packets that use serial communication [29].

Smart card–based applications work in master–slave fashion (as shown in Figure 2.2). A remote smart card–based application, also known as a host application, sends a command to the reader via middleware in order to get the required information. The middleware is any kind of software or hardware that acts as a link of communication between the card and the reader. The reader is connected with the middleware through RS 232

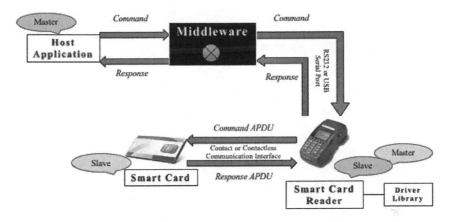

FIGURE 2.2   Working of smart cards.

or Universal Serial Bus (USB). The application in this scenario works as a master, whereas the reader acts as a slave. The reader then sends command APDU to the smart card for fetching the card holder–specific information. Command APDU contains a default header along with data. The reader in this case acts as master and the card acts as slave. The card provides the required information by sending response APDUs. The response APDU contains requested data along with compulsory status bytes. The reader in turn sends this information to the remote application for further processing. Smart cards may contain an operating system to implement some standard commands.

2.4 CONCLUSION

In this chapter, we presented a detailed taxonomy of smart cards based on various aspects, including configuration, security features, communication interface, type of embedded components, nature of application, operating system, and so forth, and discussed their various aspects including hardware and software configurations, key applications, and so forth. In a later section, we discussed in detail how a smart card–based system works, including how various entities, such as the remote host application, middleware, smart card reader, and smart card, interact with each other.

In the next chapter, we will discuss various hardware- and software-level security attacks on smart cards.

REFERENCES

1. Gupta, B. B., & Quamara, M. (2018). A taxonomy of various attacks on smart card–based applications and countermeasures. *Concurrency and Computation: Practice and Experience*, e4993.
2. Arlington, D. L., Cole, J. M., Hazelzet, B. G., Krolak, D. J., Li, H. H., Oza, B. J., & Weaver, A. F. (1989). U.S. Patent No. 4,888,773. Washington, DC: U.S. Patent and Trademark Office.
3. Asnaashari, M., Shah, R. D., Prevost, S., & Krishna, K. (2012). U.S. Patent No. 8,286,883. Washington, DC: U.S. Patent and Trademark Office.
4. Chikouche, N., Cherif, F., & Benmohammed, M. (2012). An authentication protocol based on combined RFID-biometric system RFID-biometric system. *International Journal of Advanced Computer Science and Applications*, *3*(4), 62–67.
5. Devaux, F., & Perrot, D. (2002). U.S. Patent No. 6,484,937. Washington, DC: U.S. Patent and Trademark Office.
6. Soltesz, J. A., & Keller, R. (1998). U.S. Patent No. 5,756,978. Washington, DC: U.S. Patent and Trademark Office.
7. Grimonprez, G., & Paradinas, P. (1995). U.S. Patent No. 5,473,690. Washington, DC: U.S. Patent and Trademark Office.
8. Halawani, T., & Mohandes, M. (2003, December). Smart card for smart campus: KFUPM case study. In *Electronics, Circuits and Systems, 2003. ICECS 2003. Proceedings of the 2003 10th IEEE International Conference*, *3*, 1252–1255.
9. Naccache, D., & M'Raihi, D. (1996). Cryptographic smart cards. *IEEE Micro*, *16*(3), 14–24.
10. Kocher, P. C., Jaffe, J. M., & Jun, B. C. (2001). U.S. Patent No. 6,278,783. Washington, DC: U.S. Patent and Trademark Office.
11. Woodbury, A. D., Bailey, D. V., & Paar, C. (2000). Elliptic curve cryptography on smart cards without coprocessors. In *Smart card research and advanced applications* (pp. 71–92). Boston, MA: Springer.
12. Secure Technology Alliance. (2015). INSIDE contactless offers free, downloadable, open NFC API and source code on SourceForge. Retrieved from https://www.securetechalliance.org/inside-contactless-offers-free-downloadable-open-nfc-api-and-source-code-on-sourceforge/
13. Bashan, O., Itay, N., Gazit, N., & Haroosh, Y. (2016). U.S. Patent No. 9,342,778. Washington, DC: U.S. Patent and Trademark Office.
14. Finn, D., Conneely, P. G., Czornack, J. T., Ummenhofer, K., & Lotya, M. (2015). U.S. Patent No. 9,033,250. Washington, DC: U.S. Patent and Trademark Office.
15. Kayanakis, G., Mathieu, C., & Delenne, S. (2002). U.S. Patent No. 6,406,935. Washington, DC: U.S. Patent and Trademark Office.
16. Doyle, R., Hind, J., & Peters, M. (2002). U.S. Patent Application No. 09/764,844. Washington, DC: U.S. Patent and Trademark Office.
17. Aussel, J. (2007). Smart cards and digital identity. *Telektronikk*, *103*(3/4), 66.
18. Moon, D., Lee, S., & Chung, Y. (2009). Configurable fuzzy fingerprint vault for Match-on-Card system. *IEICE Electronics Express*, *6*(14), 993–999.

19. Krawczewicz, M. (2015). U.S. Patent No. 9,122,964. Washington, DC: U.S. Patent and Trademark Office.
20. Asanoma, T., Fukushima, S., Ishihara, T., & Kitaori, S. (2003). U.S. Patent Application No. 10/237,068. Washington, DC: U.S. Patent and Trademark Office.
21. Shy, O., & Tarkka, J. (2002). The market for electronic cash cards. *Journal of Money, Credit and Banking, 2*, 299–314.
22. Mullen, J. D., & Reutzel, W. (2019). U.S. Patent Application No. 10/169,692. Washington, DC: U.S. Patent and Trademark Office.
23. Ghosh, S. K. (2016). U.S. Patent No. 9,286,481. Washington, DC: U.S. Patent and Trademark Office.
24. Vayssiere, J. J. P. (2007). U.S. Patent No. 7,270,276. Washington, DC: U.S. Patent and Trademark Office.
25. Hobson, C. L., & Hussain, S. M. (2013). U.S. Patent No. 8,484,134. Washington, DC: U.S. Patent and Trademark Office.
26. Hansmann, U., Nicklous, M. S., Schäck, T., Schneider, A., & Seliger, F. (2012). *Smart card application development using Java.* New York, NY: Springer Science & Business Media.
27. Sauveron, D. (2009). Multiapplication smart card: Towards an open smart card? *Information Security Technical Report, 14*(2), 70–78.
28. SecureIDNews. (2018). New smart card for Microsoft Minidriver environments hits market. Retrieved from https://www.secureidnews.com/news-item/new-smart-card-for-microsoft-minidriver-environments-hits-market/
29. Gkaniatsou, A., McNeill, F., Bundy, A., Steel, G., Focardi, R., & Bozzato, C. (2015, December). Getting to know your card: Reverse-engineering the smart-card application protocol data unit. In *Proceedings of the 31st Annual Computer Security Applications Conference* (pp. 441–450). Retrieved from https://dl.acm.org/citation.cfm?doid=2818000.2818020

Hardware-Level Security Attacks and Logical Threats in Smart Cards

3

3.1 INTRODUCTION

Quickly developing information systems seek interest of the developers for effective administration and safety efforts. The smart card is an embedded microchip innovation that has been relied upon to provide physical access to the individuals and to facilitate data transfer in a multitude of transactions and applications in the private, public, or government sectors. These cards have advanced from simple memory-based gadgets to perplexing and ground-breaking processing units with committed equipment and programming parts. These segments work together to accomplish a specific purpose.

However, progressive utilization of this technology has made it defenseless against countless assaults of specific or general nature. In this chapter, we discuss the different security threats on the hardware and software segments of smart cards in detail and present appropriate countermeasures for these attacks.

3.2 HARDWARE-LEVEL SECURITY ATTACKS

Hardware-level attacks target the microprocessor chip in smart cards. Figure 3.1 outlines some of the hardware-level security attack types that are briefly discussed in the following subsections.

3.2.1 Invasive or Active Attacks

These attacks involve the use of physical mechanisms to execute direct tampering with the smart cards, and hence, they are also known as active or physical attacks. The attacker penetrates the smart card to obtain physical access to the microprocessor chip embedded in it to perform detailed analysis. The attacker further examines the vulnerabilities associated with the

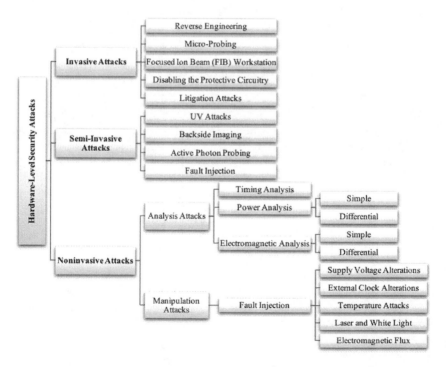

FIGURE 3.1   Hardware-level security attacks on smart cards.

chip that can be exploited to manipulate the normal and expected working of the card. Limited initial knowledge is required to conduct these attacks. However, extensive resources such as special equipment and costly tools are required to perform them. Moreover, significant time is required to carry out these attacks.

Invasive attack methodologies can be of manual or optical nature and are discussed below:

1. **Reverse engineering**—In reverse engineering, smart card de-packaging is done to remove the micro-processor chip, which then undergoes complete systematic analysis. On obtaining the chip from the plastic card, an attacker can use an optical microscope to recognize different functional or processing modules, data lines, address lines, and so on. Afterward, layout of the chip can be redesigned by observing the successive layers of the smart card. The details of the underlying design of the card are acquired to determine the working of the chip or a specific block to find and control the possible weaknesses in the chip. The card's integrity is compromised by accessing the values stored in the memory.

   Numerous research has been done to develop reverse engineering methodologies and to understand their overall effectiveness. The Computer Laboratory at the University of Cambridge and Quo Vadis Labs in London developed a technique for reverse engineering the smart card circuit chip [1]. This technique is capable of extracting the content of the Flash electrically erasable programmable read-only memory (EEPROM) through scanning electron microscopy (SEM) and standard image processing techniques. Lanet et al. [2] proposed a disassembler based on natural language recognition and heuristics for reverse engineering a Java Card memory dump. Quadir et al. [3] present a survey on the available reverse engineering and anti–reverse engineering methodologies on the electronic chips.

2. **Micro-probing**—In this technique, an attacker establishes an electrical contact with the bus lines by placing micro-probe needles on them between the blocks of the chip without causing any physical damage to them. This helps the attacker to monitor the bus signals or the data moving across the blocks on an oscilloscope and to extract the sensitive information out of it by forming new channels. This sensitive information may comprise cryptographic keys, program code, or operating system files present in the nonvolatile memory (read-only memory [ROM]) [4]. An amplifier is used via which the probe is connected to a digital signal processor card for

recording the processor's signals and providing Input/Output (I/O), power, clock, and reset signals required for operating the processor via pins [5].

3. **Focused ion beam (FIB) workstation**—A metallic defense grid possessing the properties below the wavelength of visible light is sometimes present at the top level for hiding the bus signals [6]. FIB workstations can be used to develop and ruin the tracks on the smart card chip's surface to extract the signals. Chip material can be removed with great resolution in case of high beam current. These days, FIB workstations are used by the attackers for simplifying the manual probing of poly-silicon lines and deep metals.

   The electron beam tester (EBT) is another commonly used particle beam tool. It is a scanning electron microscope with voltage contrast function that has the ability to measure waveforms having several gigahertz of bandwidth. However, the electron beam is continuously focused on a single spot when used in real-time voltage contrast mode. A noisy and blurred stream of secondary electrons is recorded, and signal bandwidth is restricted to a few megahertz. EBTs can be used for real-time recording of all the bus lines if the microprocessor can be made to generate periodic signals by constantly executing the same transaction at the time of measurement or if the clock frequency of the target microprocessor chip can be reduced below 100 kHz [7]. Infrared lasers can also be used for this purpose.

4. **Other techniques**—Smart cards may contain an alarm circuit that works in unusual events or a protective circuit including access control matrices in order to restrict access for some areas in the memory using a personal identification number (PIN) or passwords [8]. Laser light can be used to shoot away these circuits. Another type of attack or illegal methodology, known as litigation attack, involves obtaining the patent of the card design through infringement and using the legal discovery process for obtaining the design details [9].

3.2.2 Semi-Invasive Attacks

These attacks allow attackers to invade the microprocessor chip's security without any physical modification of the chip [6]. They involve de-packaging or exposure of the chip's surface and ensure that no electrical contact is made with the metallic layer of the chip, and thus, they cause no physical damage to the silicon. In comparison to noninvasive attacks, these attacks are complex to perform. These attacks are not specific to modern feature size chips because they are applied over the whole transistor within the chip. Appropriate computing tactics can be used to automate these attacks, and various tools are used individually or together to conduct them. Different methods for performing these attacks are discussed below:

1. **Ultraviolet (UV) attacks**—Most of the UV attacks require de-capsulation of the smart card chip. These can be conducted on different UV-EPROM and one-time programmable microcontrollers, because they do not have required protection to resist such attacks. While conducting these attacks, two phases are involved— identifying the location of the fuse on the chip and using UV light to reset it to an unprotected state. To locate the fuse, methods such as laser light scanning, UV light, reverse engineering, or optical fault injection can be used [10]. However, the fuse cannot be erased before the program memory because the layout may be in such a way that it might be embedded into the memory array or sharing the same area with the memory. Hence, either some opaque material should be used to cover the memory or a microscope and UV laser can be used for selective erasing of the fuse. Another enhanced technique of UV-based attacks is the toothpick attack, which is characterized by optical fault induction as well as other unknown attacks [11]. It involves using an ordinary marker pen to paint the areas on the chip surface and scratching the desired area using a wooden toothpick.

2. **Backside imaging techniques**—These techniques involve analyzing the microprocessor chip by visually observing it under a microscope [12]. These attacks can be used for extracting the content from masked ROM, failure analysis involving locating the failures in transistors and interconnections, and navigation during FIB process.

3. **Active photon probing**—A beam of coherent light or laser can produce the same effect on semiconductor chips as ionizing radiation, such as cosmic rays, x-rays, and so on [12]. When energy of the photons exceeds the semiconductor band gap, laser light causes ionization of the integrated chip's semiconductor regions, which results in the generation of electron-hole pairs. This attack is called active photon probing. As the transistors in modern semiconductor chips become thinner, visible light (such as green or red lasers) with high frequency can be used for the same purpose because the photon absorption rate is high. The size of the device also determines the level of ionization. Lesser energy is required to achieve the same level of ionization in smaller devices. This technique can be used to extract the content stored in the memory of the smart card.

4. **Fault injection**—With the illumination of the target resistor, current flows in it, which can cause induction of transient faults [13]. These attacks can be carried out easily without requiring any expensive laser equipment. To disrupt the normal control flow of the microprocessor chip, errors can be introduced in the cryptographic algorithms or processing using optical probing. Memory content can also be extracted or modified using optical probing. On exposure of the semiconductor chip to an intense light source, the state of the memory cell changes. The memory address map can also be reverse engineered using this attack. An attacker can introduce conditional branches in the smart card code to be interpreted wrongly. For instance, number of rounds in a block cipher can be reduced to one or two to reduce the complexity of the key recovery process [14].

3.2.3 Noninvasive Attacks

These attacks are characterized by the extraction of the key information without tampering of the card chip (i.e., no damage is caused to the plastic body or the microprocessor chip of the smart card) [15]. Normal processing of any command is accompanied by leakage of some information. The attacker observes and uses this information for deducing the internal functioning of the device. These attacks are also known as side channel attacks and are used to understand how the properties of the device are changed while processing different types of information. Low-cost equipment is used to obtain the required detailed knowledge of the embedded software and microprocessor chip. No evidence of physical tampering is left behind, which makes it difficult to detect them, and hence, these attacks possess the greatest threat of all. For instance, validity of a stolen secret key cannot be revoked before misuse because the owner of the key is not aware it has been stolen [16]. These attacks are not card specific and are easily reproducible because the software designed for a particular card type can be easily regenerated for another within a short span. Moreover, the attacker has full control over the clock lines and power supply.

Different noninvasive attack mechanisms can be divided into two categories: analysis based and manipulation based. Analysis-based techniques (also known as passive attacks) involve an attacker observing the behavior of the electronic circuitry during the ongoing transactions. These include timing analysis, power analysis, and electromagnetic analysis. Unlike analysis-based techniques, manipulation-based techniques, such as fault injection, involve modification of parameters of the electronic circuit. These techniques are described as follows:

1. **Timing analysis**—These attacks deal with determining the overall time taken to carry out an operation by a processing unit. They involve identifying the data-dependent time taken in order to extract the key information [17, 18]. An adversary can observe the time at which the reader sends the command to the smart card and the time at which it gets the corresponding response from the card. Once it is done, the overall time taken for the execution of the command can be determined by taking the difference between the two. Use of proprietary readers, logic analyzers, and an oscilloscope can make this attack more effective because more precise timings can be obtained.

2. **Power analysis**—This is another type of a side channel attack in which an adversary monitors the instantaneous power consumption of a microprocessor during the execution of cryptographic operations. For this purpose, a serial circuit consisting of a power supply or ground, smart card, and resistor is created, and the voltage difference across the resistor is measured using an oscilloscope [19]. This voltage difference provides information about the internal functioning of the microprocessor within the smart card.

   Power analysis attacks can be categorized into two groups: simple power analysis (SPA) and differential power analysis (DPA) [20]. In SPA attacks, a cryptographic algorithm is supplied with the input to determine the patterns within the obtained power consumption readings of the system. These are then used by an attacker to determine the exact location of the functional logic within the commands under execution because different levels of power consumption are required by different functions for execution. For example, the Data Encryption Standard (DES) algorithm under execution involves repetition of 16 rounds of computation, the corresponding pattern of which is observed being repeated 16 times in power consumption measurements. These observations do not necessarily provide any immediate apparent information but can help in improving the impact of other attacks. SPA helps in understanding the sequence of operations involved in execution and can break the cryptographic implementations in which sequence of execution relies on the data under processing. In addition, SPA can be used to break the implementations based on the Rivest-Shamir-Adleman (RSA) algorithm. This involves analyzing the difference between squaring and multiplication operations, by which information related to the private key can be deduced.

In DPA, differences between executions of data-dependent power emissions are used to obtain the private keys. Unlike SPA, which involves use of a visual inspection technique to identify the relative power variations, DPA is a statistical analysis–based technique for extracting the private information. In addition, these attacks do not require detailed information about the implementation of the algorithm.

3. **Electromagnetic analysis**—Electromagnetic analysis involves measuring the instantaneous electromagnetic emissions using probes when a cryptographic algorithm is under execution [21]. Different levels of electromagnetic radiation are emitted from different blocks. Probes with size equivalent to the chip's features are placed over a given feature on the chip to detect a strong electromagnetic signal while noisy signals from other areas of the chip are excluded. Amplifiers are used for to help the oscilloscope detect the emitted signals. Electromagnetic analysis can be of two types: simple electromagnetic analysis (SEMA) and differential electromagnetic analysis (DEMA) [19]. SEMA involves analysis of the acquired information individually, whereas DEMA involves performing statistical analysis of the obtained data.

4. **Fault injection**—Other than light, different means exist for injecting faults. For example, transients can be introduced into clock lines or power supplies. This leads to malfunctioning or failure of the smart card chip in a predictable manner. This attack, also known as a glitch attack, can cause algorithm- and execution-dependent effects, such as data randomization, resetting of data by forcing the data to the blank state, instruction manipulation, removal of functions, and loop breaks. For instance, security checks can be bypassed. From the initial observation on faults, it can be concluded that the packaging material of the chip constitutes different elements (e.g., uranium-235, uranium-238, and thorium-230 residues) that produce electromagnetic particles (alpha particles) that are strong enough to cause manipulation of the data bits stored in the volatile memory (random access memory [RAM]). An example that is related to cryptographic algorithms is presence of faults during the use of the Chinese Remainder Theorem (CRT) for computing RSA signature [22]. This can lead to breach of information privacy. There are various mechanisms that can be adopted to inject faults (permanent or transient) in the smart card microprocessor chips. They are listed below [23, 24].

Alterations in supply voltage—Alterations in supply voltage may cause the microprocessor to misinterpret the instructions or skip the instructions during computations.

Alterations in external clock—The clock frequency can be manipulated to cause instructions to be missed or data items to be misread by the microprocessor. It can also lead to violation of set-up time.

Temperature attacks—The desired temperature conditions for the working of smart card systems can be varied in a fashion causing abnormal heating of the chip accompanied by random alterations in the memory cells. Overheating may also lead to permanent damage of the chip. Moreover, the threshold values of the temperature associated with the read and write operations can be changed, resulting in conflict and other attacks based on the same.

Laser light—Photoelectric effect involves current induction when light is made to strike the metal surface of the semiconductor chip. If the intensity of the light is high enough, as in case of laser light, it can induce faults on the chip's circuit and can ensure high precision and granularity of the level of a single memory cell. However, expensive equipment is required for carrying out this attack.

White light—White light can be used as an inexpensive alternative to laser light for fault induction. It differs from laser light in that it is nondirectional, which makes it difficult to irradiate the minute portions of the microprocessor chip.

Electromagnetic flux—In microprocessors that lack security, eddy currents can be made strong by using an electromagnetic probe and high-voltage pulse generator to change the data values stored in RAM.

3.3 SOFTWARE-LEVEL SECURITY ATTACKS

Smart cards can be described as small computers with embedded software that are vulnerable to the presence of hidden malware or bugs. Software-level attacks (or logical attacks) aim to exploit these bugs and can lead to unexpected functioning of the smart cards or software implementation of corresponding applications. The malware can also introduce nonmalicious flaws in the software as side effects. These attacks are easy to reproduce using cheap

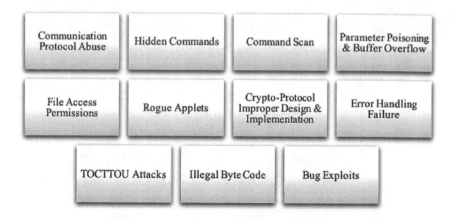

FIGURE 3.2   Logical threats on smart card–based applications.

equipment. Possible software-level attacks are summarized in Figure 3.2 and are described below [25–31].

1. Communication protocol abuse—Communication protocols facilitate data handling and error recovery by establishing communication and information exchange between the smart card and the reader. Messages in an ongoing transmission can be manipulated as per the requirement by exploiting the features of the communication protocol to reveal the secret information being exchanged.

2. Hidden commands—Smart card reader gives certain commands to direct the overall operations that are executed by the operating system present on the card. These demands include SELECT, READ, UPDATE, AUTHENTICATE, VERIFY, and so forth. Only a few of them are actually used in practical usage. The commands that are a part of the initialization phase or from any precious application can be misapplied to retrieve confidential information or to manipulate the data.

3. Command scan—An attacker can use Command Scan Service Routine (CSSR) for scanning the command buffer in unauthorized way. The results of the scan are then analyzed to determine the details associated with the command in execution and to manipulate its purpose.

4. Parameter poisoning and buffer overflow—Requests are specified by the parameters associated with the commands. In some cases, unexpected results are generated when a value or length

associated with the parameter, which is not allowed, is misconceived instead of dismissed. For instance, a file read request command may comprise a parameter value that may exceed the actual or acceptable size.

5. File access permissions—The nested file system in the smart card contains files that have some associated permissions. To ensure protection of the file data, these access permissions define required security mechanisms that perform credential verification and authentication for each command related to file access. The access permissions may become confused when multiple different applications are sending requests to access the same file within a single session and may allow a higher level of access than needed.

6. Rogue applets—Rogue and malicious applets make multiapplication smart cards susceptible to various security breaches. For instance, applets affected by a Trojan horse can be installed to compromise the security of the legitimate applications that are supported by the smart card and can steal the confidential information.

7. Crypto-protocol improper design and implementation—Crypto-protocols are associated with the execution of cryptographic operations during smart card–based transactions. These are executed in hardware, and their execution is controlled by software programs. Improper modeling and execution of these protocols can cause breach in confidentiality and various security attacks and exploits, including replay and relay attacks. Some of the possible threats include bugs in random number generators and proprietary algorithms. Key management software that deals with key generation, key storage, key usage and exchange, and stored procedures can also be exploited by the malicious adversaries.

8. Error handling failure—Smart card system software may have the inadvertent flaw of the absence of adequate software design for handling exceptional situations.

9. Time-of-check-to-time-of-use (TOCTTOU) attacks—These can be defined as a race condition between the time of check of the security resource or credentials and the time of their use. For instance, an improper balance check in financial applications can lead to improper results.

10. Illegal byte code—Illegal or ill-typed byte codes can lead to type confusion in order to obtain illegal access to the smart card memory. In the absence of a byte code verifier, which is usually optional in smart cards, this attack cannot be prevented. It can also lead to bypassing of the run-time security measures of a firewall.

11. Bug exploits—Software-based attacks also target bugs present in the application software, cryptographic software, communication platform, and so forth, to exploit them in order to steal the sensitive information.

3.4 COUNTERMEASURES

In this section, we discuss various countermeasures for the security attacks discussed in the previous section.

3.4.1 Countermeasures for Hardware-Level Security Attacks

Figure 3.3 outlines some of the effective countermeasures for hardware-level security attacks on smart cards. A brief discussion of these measures is provided in the following subsections.

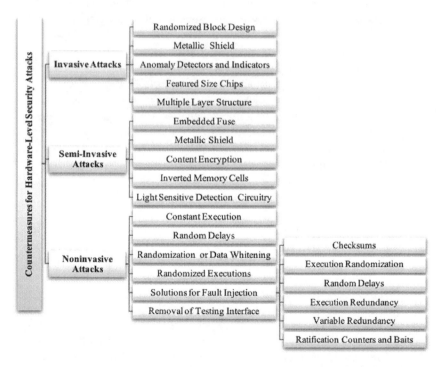

FIGURE 3.3   Countermeasures for hardware-level security attacks.

3.4.1.1 Countermeasures for Invasive Attacks

Following are some of the countermeasures for invasive attacks.

1. **Randomized or scrambled block design**—The critical blocks that are present on the microprocessor card chip include memory, data buses, address buses, and so forth. Design of these blocks can be laid out in a randomized way so as to make the reverse engineering attacks difficult to carry out. In other words, it can be defined as the introduction of variability in the block design. To conceal the chip design mechanism against probing techniques, embedded software can be obscured. However, this technique can be used for larger blocks, such as EEPROM and ROM, because it increases the size of these blocks. Glue logic is another variant of this technique in which customized logical and digital circuitry can be used to hide the actual functionality of the chip [32]. It prevents cloning using a reverse engineering attack.

2. **Metallic shield**—To prevent visual or physical identification using reverse engineering attacks, an additional metallic layer that does not allow the flow of electric signals through it can be added over the functional layers of the microprocessor chip or over the whole chip [33]. Security-intensive critical blocks can be protected using this technique. However, this layer is vulnerable to chemicals such as hydrofluoric (HF) acid, which can be used to easily remove this layer. To prevent this reaction, acetone can be used on the chip's surface.

3. **Anomaly detectors and indicators**—To detect the unanticipated environmental situations or unusual events associated with the voltage supply or external clock and to generate alerts for these situations, anomaly detectors and indicators can be embedded on the smart card circuit [34, 35]. As a response, a memory reset is initiated by the smart card for protecting the data, and the system may also go into infinite loop. In some cases, if the unusual condition is not handled, the system may come to a halt. Various types of sensors can be used for such cases including heat detectors, light intensity sensors, clock frequency sensors, temperature sensors, over- or undervoltage detectors, and so on. For instance, these sensors produce signals when the value of an operational parameter crosses the threshold value defined for it for the correct functioning of the chip.

4. **Other techniques**—Feature-size chips are becoming increasingly popular due to their compact size and advanced design. These are generally difficult to be analyzed by standard microscopes. In

addition, a multilayered structure can be adopted in the card design, which involves placing the sensitive connections such as the data buses, beneath the layers that contain less sensitive connections.

3.4.1.2 Countermeasures for Semi-Invasive Attacks

Following are some of the countermeasures against semi-invasive attacks.

1. **Embedded fuse**—If in the circuitry of the smart card the fuse is present at enough distance from the programmable memory, opaque material such as duct tape can be used to cover the memory to locate the fuse easily. To prevent UV attacks in such cases, the fuse can be embedded within the programmable memory array, which would make it difficult to locate.
2. **Metallic shield**—For protecting the fuse from reset by UV attacks, a metallic layered covering can be placed on top of it to protect it from being identified and located. For instance, this technique can be found with many 14- or 16-bit core one-time programmable peripheral interface controller (OTP-PIC) microcontrollers.
3. **Other techniques**—Encryption techniques can ensure data confidentiality and integrity even in case of chip exposure. For protection against UV attacks, less sensitive inverted memory cells can also be used. In addition, detection circuitry that is sensitive to light can be used against UV attacks.

3.4.1.3 Countermeasures for Noninvasive Attacks

A number of countermeasures have been developed for the protection of cryptographic algorithms against noninvasive attacks; these are described below.

1. **Constant execution**—This technique involves execution of a cryptographic algorithm that processes secret information in a fixed time duration, which can prevent an attacker from making any inferences from the secret information through data-dependent timing analysis or SPA attacks of the card's chip. When different secret information is provided as input to the algorithm in execution, the corresponding power measurements would not contain directly interpretable information. However, if the algorithm takes different times to execute the same piece of information, it could possibly be due to the dummy function in the code. The same is also reflected in the power consumption readings.

2. **Random delays or time equalization**—This technique is characterized by the introduction of dummy code or function at any point in the cryptographic algorithm under execution. Because this code takes varying amounts of time for execution, it is difficult for the attacker to interpret any valid secret information through power or timing analysis attacks. In other words, this technique involves randomly shifting the execution timings of operations. Covert timing channels (storage or timing) can be used during data transmission for randomizing the silence periods [36].

3. **Randomization or data whitening**—In this technique, a random value known as a mask is used for masking the stored data values in the memory, and hence, it is also known as data masking or binding. The aim is to protect the sensitive information in the memory from any direct interpretations [37]. For one execution, the manipulation is kept the same but is typically varied for further rounds. For example, performing an XOR operation on a data value a and a random mask m will hide the key value of a, making it difficult for the attacker to directly interpret the same. However, the result is reversible in order to obtain the original data values. Data re-encryption techniques can also be employed for hiding the access patterns that involve confusing the storage location of the data that is being accessed in every cycle, also termed *oblivious RAM* (ORAM) [38].

4. **Randomized executions**—Randomized executions involve performing randomized manipulation of data using nondeterministic processors to prevent the attacker from knowing what is being manipulated at a given instance.

5. **Solutions for fault injection**—The methods that we have discussed so far fulfill the goal of maintaining integrity, which lays the foundation for the countermeasures against fault injection attacks on smart cards. However, an appropriate application-level analysis is necessary for determining the preventive techniques against fault injection. Following are some of the existing solutions from the literature.

   Checksums—Checksums are used for detecting any unwanted modification of the data bits or key information due to faults.

   Execution randomization—This technique involves manipulation of the order of execution of instructions to make it difficult for an attacker to predict the ongoing operations in a given machine cycle.

   Random delays—Random delays involve introduction of deliberate delays in order to increase the overall time required for conducting the attacks.

Execution redundancy—This involves executing an algorithm in a repeated fashion and comparing the successive results to verify its correctness. This approach is typically employed in scenarios where function execution yields different results at different times in order to prevent an adversary introducing similar faults in every execution.

Variable redundancy—This involves three different tasks: generation of the same variable in the memory of the smart card, performing testing over its value, and modifying it.

Ratification counters and baits—In this technique, functioning of the microprocessor chip comes to halt when a fault attack is detected, which prevents an adversary from successfully completing the attack. Baits are small-size codes (typically less than 10 bytes) that perform certain functions, such as reading data, writing data, comparing data, addition, multiplication, XOR operation, and so forth, and test their results. In case an error is detected by them, the value of the counter in the nonvolatile memory is incremented. If this value crosses a predefined threshold (usually kept as 3), working of the microprocessor chip comes to halt.

6. **Removal of testing interface**—This approach involves physically removing the testing interface, which is used for flash memory programming and testing after card production to protect against fault injection attacks. This testing interface can be removed once the testing is done by cutting it off, which would prevent the attacker from using it and obtaining access to buses and control lines.

3.4.2 Countermeasures for Software-Level Security Attacks

The sensitivity level of logical threats is determined by the software complexity. More bugs and flaws may be introduced with increasing size of the software code. To deal with software bugs and flaws, the following strategies can be implemented (Figure 3.4).

1. **Backup methods**—Cryptographic schemes may use a backup method, such as cryptographic co-processors, for dealing with the technical problems and to improve the reliability of the software. In addition, to ensure security and to deal with malicious functions, additional measures such as access control mechanisms can be opted.

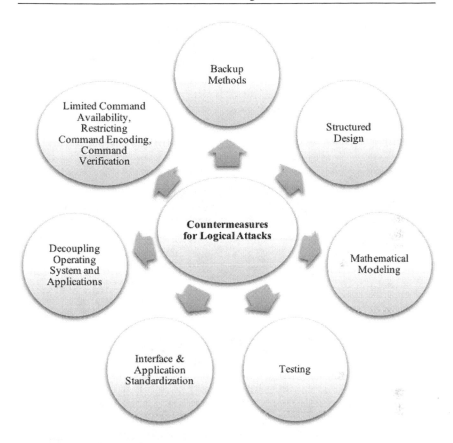

FIGURE 3.4   Countermeasures for software-level security attacks.

2. **Structured design**—To establish easy understanding and testing of the software, its functionality can be partitioned into smaller building blocks. Object-oriented language concepts (e.g., Java-based Card Operating System) can also be employed to improve the security.

3. **Mathematical modeling**—To validate the functionality of the software and improve the security of its functional building blocks, mathematical models, such as the random oracle model, RSA, and so forth, can be used.

4. **Testing**—Testing involves mechanisms that are consistently executed during different stages of the software design and development process in order to find and fix the bugs to prevent security flaws. Experimental validation of the implementation and testing of file access mechanisms should be ensured.

5. **Interface and application standardization**—Reuse of software that has already undergone the rigorous process of validation reduces the likelihood of vulnerabilities and flaws, making the process of security policy implementation easier and more effective.
6. **Decoupling operating system and applications**—To ensure that the application and operating system residing over the smart card perform their respective tasks in an independent and autonomous fashion, these should be allocated with separate memory. This also ensures that if one of these become the target of the security attacks, the other can work regardless of the attack.
7. **Solutions for command scan attacks**—To prevent command scan attacks, restrictions can be made on the availability of commands to the applications. Moreover, regulating the command encoding and its verification in an appropriate manner can prevent these attacks.

3.5 CONCLUSION

In this chapter, we discussed various attacks on the hardware and software segments of smart cards, along with appropriate countermeasures for these attacks.

In the next chapter, we will look into various security threats and attacks associated with data stored or transmitted in smart card–based systems and applications.

REFERENCES

1. Courbon, F., Skorobogatov, S., & Woods, C. (2016, November). Reverse engineering flash EEPROM memories using scanning electron microscopy. In *International Conference on Smart Card Research and Advanced Applications* (pp. 57–72). Cham, Switzerland: Springer.
2. Lanet, J. L., Bouffard, G., Lamrani, R., Chakra, R., Mestiri, A., Monsif, M., & Fandi, A. (2014, November). Memory forensics of a Java card dump. In *International Conference on Smart Card Research and Advanced Applications* (pp. 3–17). Cham, Switzerland: Springer.

3. Quadir, S. E., Chen, J., Forte, D., Asadizanjani, N., Shahbazmohamadi, S., Wang, L., . . . Tehranipoor, M. (2016). A survey on chip to system reverse engineering. *ACM Journal on Emerging Technologies in Computing Systems (JETC)*, *13*(1), 6.
4. Skorobogatov, S. (2017, August). How microprobing can attack encrypted memory. In *2017 Euromicro Conference on Digital System Design (DSD)* (pp. 244–251). IEEE. Retrieved from https://www.researchgate.net/publication/320089578_How_Microprobing_Can_Attack_Encrypted_Memory
5. Shi, Q., Forte, D., & Tehranipoor, M. M. (2017). Analyzing circuit layout to probing attack. In *Hardware IP security and trust* (pp. 73–98). Cham, Switzerland: Springer.
6. Gupta, B. B., & Quamara, M. (2018). A taxonomy of various attacks on smart card–based applications and countermeasures. *Concurrency and Computation: Practice and Experience*, e4993. Retrieved from https://onlinelibrary.wiley.com/doi/abs/10.1002/cpe.4993
7. Thong, J. T. (Ed.). (2013). *Electron beam testing technology*. New York, NY: Springer Science & Business Media.
8. Kömmerling, O., & Kuhn, M. G. (1999). Design principles for tamper-resistant smartcard processors. *Smartcard*, *99*, 9–20.
9. Moore, S., Anderson, R., Cunningham, P., Mullins, R., & Taylor, G. (2002, April). Improving smart card security using self-timed circuits. In *Asynchronous Circuits and Systems, 2002. Proceedings. Eighth International Symposium on* (pp. 211–218). IEEE.
10. Skorobogatov, S. P., & Anderson, R. J. (2002, August). Optical fault induction attacks. In *International Workshop on Cryptographic Hardware and embedded Systems* (pp. 2–12). Berlin, Germany: Springer.
11. Skorobogatov, S. (2012). Physical attacks and tamper resistance. In *Introduction to hardware security and trust* (pp. 143–173). New York, NY: Springer.
12. Skorobogatov, S. P. (2005). *Semi-invasive attacks: A new approach to hardware security analysis* (Doctoral dissertation). Cambridge, United Kingdom: University of Cambridge.
13. Cai, F., Bai, G., Liu, H., & Hu, X. (2016, June). Optical fault injection attacks for flash memory of smartcards. In *2016 6th International Conference on Electronics Information and Emergency Communication (ICEIEC)* (pp. 46–50). IEEE.
14. Anderson, R., & Kuhn, M. (1997, April). Low cost attacks on tamper resistant devices. In *International Workshop on Security Protocols* (pp. 125–136). Berlin, Germany: Springer.
15. Moein, S., Gulliver, T. A., Gebali, F., & Alkandari, A. (2017). Hardware attack mitigation techniques analysis. *International Journal of Information Security*, *7*(1), 9–28.
16. Li, Y., Chen, M., & Wang, J. (2016, May). Introduction to side-channel attacks and fault attacks. In *2016 Asia-Pacific International Symposium on Electromagnetic Compatibility (APEMC)* (Vol. 1, pp. 573–575). IEEE.
17. Brumley, D., & Boneh, D. (2005). Remote timing attacks are practical. *Computer Networks*, *48*(5), 701–716.
18. Kocher, P. C. (1996, August). Timing attacks on implementations of Diffie-Hellman, RSA, DSS, and other systems. In *Annual International Cryptology Conference* (pp. 104–113). Berlin, Germany: Springer.

19. Mahanta, H. J., Azad, A. K., & Khan, A. K. (2015, January). Power analysis attack: A vulnerability to smart card security. In *2015 International Conference on Signal Processing and Communication Engineering Systems* (pp. 506–510). IEEE.

20. Ambrose, C., Bos, J. W., Fay, B., Joye, M., Lochter, M., & Murray, B. (2018, April). Differential attacks on deterministic signatures. In *Cryptographers' Track at the RSA Conference* (pp. 339–353). Cham, Switzerland: Springer.

21. Longo, J., De Mulder, E., Page, D., & Tunstall, M. (2015, September). SoC it to EM: Electromagnetic side-channel attacks on a complex system-on-chip. In *International Workshop on Cryptographic Hardware and Embedded Systems* (pp. 620–640). Berlin, Germany: Springer.

22. Schmidt, J. M., & Hutter, M. (2007). Optical and EM fault-attacks on CRT-based RSA: Concrete results (pp. 61–67). Retrieved from https://online.tugraz.at/tug_online/voe_main2.getvolltext?pCurrPk=32877

23. Kim, C. H., & Quisquater, J. J. (2007). Faults, injection methods, and fault attacks. *IEEE Design & Test of Computers*, 24(6), 544–545.

24. Bar-El, H., Choukri, H., Naccache, D., Tunstall, M., & Whelan, C. (2006). The sorcerer's apprentice guide to fault attacks. *Proceedings of the IEEE*, 94(2), 370–382.

25. Witteman, M. (2002). Advances in smartcard security. *Information Security Bulletin*, 7(2002), 11–22.

26. Iguchi-Cartigny, J., & Lanet, J. L. (2010). Developing a Trojan applets in a smart card. *Journal in Computer Virology*, 6(4), 343–351.

27. Kfir, Z., & Wool, A. (2005, September). Picking virtual pockets using relay attacks on contactless smartcard. In *Security and Privacy for Emerging Areas in Communications Networks, 2005. SecureComm 2005. First International Conference on* (pp. 47–58). IEEE.

28. Potter, B., & McGraw, G. (2004). Software security testing. *IEEE Security & Privacy*, 2(5), 81–85.

29. Calafato, A., & Markantonakis, K. (n.d.). *Smart cards are getting smarter.* Retrieved from http://docs.media.bitpipe.com/io_10x/io_102267/item_674000/RH%20article%206%20smart%20cards.pdf

30. Volokitin, S., & Poll, E. (2016, November). Logical attacks on secured containers of the Java Card platform. In *International Conference on Smart Card Research and Advanced Applications* (pp. 122–136). Cham, Switzerland: Springer.

31. Laugier, B., & Razafindralambo, T. (2015, November). Misuse of frame creation to exploit stack underflow attacks on Java Card. In *International Conference on Smart Card Research and Advanced Applications* (pp. 89–104). Cham, Switzerland: Springer.

32. Moein, S., Gulliver, T. A., Gebali, F., & Alkandari, A. (2017). *Hardware attack mitigation techniques analysis.* Retrieved from https://pdfs.semanticscholar.org/40d6/b2d0d9760779347565398246f2fbd2dbcf25.pdf

33. Wang, Y., Fan, D. B., Yu, J. F., Wang, J. C., Zhang, G. H., & Zheng, Q. S. (2016). U.S. Patent No. 9,325,091. Washington, DC: U.S. Patent and Trademark Office.

34. Matranga, G., Coco, L. L., & Compagno, G. (2002). U.S. Patent No. 6,489,831. Washington, DC: U.S. Patent and Trademark Office.

35. Weiner, M., Manich, S., Rodríguez-Montañés, R., & Sigl, G. (2018). The low area probing detector as a countermeasure against invasive attacks. *IEEE Transactions on Very Large Scale Integration (VLSI) Systems*, 26(2), 392–403.

36. Venkataramani, G., Chen, J., & Doroslovacki, M. (2016). Detecting hardware covert timing channels. *IEEE Micro, 36*(5), 17–27.
37. Malina, L., Dzurenda, P., Hajny, J., & Martinasek, Z. (2018, July). Assessment of cryptography support and security on programmable smart cards. In *2018 41st International Conference on Telecommunications and Signal Processing (TSP)* (pp. 1–5). IEEE.
38. Backes, M., Herzberg, A., Kate, A., & Pryvalov, I. (2016, September). Anonymous RAM. In *European Symposium on Research in Computer Security* (pp. 344–362). Cham, Switzerland: Springer.

Data Security in Smart Cards

4

4.1 INTRODUCTION

Data are a crucial part of smart card systems and applications. Smart card–based transactions involve creation of data, exchange of data through networks, data manipulation, and data storage in the smart card memory or remote servers. The underlying applications are characterized by diversity in the data that can be typically categorized as card holder–specific data (e.g., personal identification numbers [PINs] of the users, usernames, passwords, password verifiers, secret keys used for cryptographic operations) and system and application software files (e.g., operating system files, cryptographic software files, remote database server files, communicating software).

Considering the real-time smart card–based applications that involve handling of a large amount of data transmission, storage, and processing, these data are susceptible to a wide range of security attacks, including illegitimate access, deletion, manipulations, and lack of availability to the legitimate parties, which demands the deployment of efficient data security mechanisms [1]. Moreover, implementation of complex security solutions is restricted by the resource-constrained smart cards. Data security is a broader term that spans a wide range of applications. Rapid advancements in the smart card technology keep data security concerns at the peak. These concerns typically include safe arrival of data, data privacy, conformation of the receipt of data, data integrity, and so forth. It is the responsibility of the card issuer to define all the underlying parameters associated with the system for ensuring data security. In addition, card holders are expected to use the cards issued to them in a careful manner. However, to design appropriate security mechanisms, it is crucial to understand and anticipate the security threats and risks associated with these systems and to stay ahead of the evolving security attacks. In the next section, we will discuss various data-level security attacks in the smart card–based application environment.

4.2 TYPES OF DATA-LEVEL SECURITY ATTACKS IN SMART CARDS

Some of the common security threats or attacks over data in a smart card–based application environment are outlined in Figure 4.1

4.2.1 Breach of Confidentiality

Confidentiality breach occurs when the data being transmitted between authorized entities are accessed by the adversaries in an unauthorized manner. Following are the different types of attacks associated with breach of confidentiality in the smart card–based application environment.

1. **Cryptographic key crack**—An adversary, on obtaining the secret cryptographic key, can decrypt the information that is being transmitted between the communicating entities or that is stored in the system. Moreover, it can be used to generate keys for subsequent or future communication sessions [2].
2. **Security PIN crack**—An adversary can use social engineering or brute force attacks and can breach the confidentiality of the smart card by cracking the PIN associated with the card [3].
3. **Tracing the dump communications**—Past communications can become a source of confidentiality breach because the information can be obtained and reused using session key disclosure attacks [4], co-relation attacks [5], and so forth.
4. **Illegitimate access**—Obtaining access in unauthorized manner leads to breach of confidentiality [6].
5. **Copying of database files**—This involves unauthorized copying of database files incorporating the user's credentials, password verifiers, and other such identifying information [7].

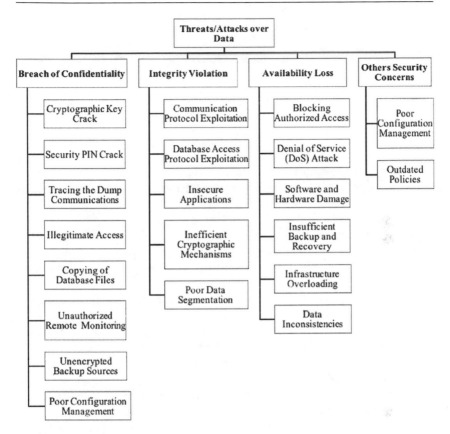

FIGURE 4.1 Data-level security attacks in smart card–based application environment.

6. **Unauthorized remote monitoring**—This involves monitoring the secret data in an ongoing transaction, including credentials and PIN. Hidden terminals can be placed for intercepting the ongoing transmission and point-of-sale (PoS) transactions. On-board terminals can also be targeted by the hackers [8].

7. **Unencrypted backup sources**—Exposure of the data stored in backup drives such as tapes, hard disks, and remote servers that are typically unencrypted can also lead to key information being revealed [9].

8. **Poor configuration management**—Poorly configured networks and devices used for a longer period can result in breach of data confidentiality [10]. Change in network configuration can have

unexpected impact, which could lead to the introduction of risks. Third-party systems connected to the core network are also a common cause of data breaches.

4.2.2 Integrity Violation

Integrity of the data is affected when the data is lost during the transmission or gets corrupted. Underlying causes of integrity violation include insecure or vulnerable applications, incompetent or outdated cryptographic techniques, and so forth. Integrity of the system is also affected when system failure occurs in the middle of an ongoing transaction.

1. **Communication protocol exploitation**—Exploitation of the flaws and vulnerabilities present in a communication protocol may allow unauthorized entities to manipulate or corrupt the data during transmission.
2. **Database access protocol exploitation**—Data stored in remote database servers can be corrupted by exploiting the flaws present in the database access protocols. For instance, SQL Slammer works by exploiting the vulnerabilities present in Microsoft's SQL server protocol to run a malicious code on remote target database servers [11].
3. **Insecure applications**—Insecure application designs and interfaces can become an underlying factor in the violation of integrity because the data entered by the user can be manipulated by adversaries using rogue application interfaces.

    Barbu et al. [12] demonstrated how ill-formed applications can be introduced in the card execution environment, which endangers the integrity of the whole platform. For instance, ill-formed applets exploit the vulnerabilities of virtual machine (VM) implementation of Java Card or bugs present in fundamental operations. Moreover, these can defeat the security controls present in the system. According to a *Business Today* article [13], a novel attack called formjacking has been developed that involves ATM skimming virtually, in which malicious codes are inserted into PoS terminals to steal the details of payment cards of shoppers. As per the statistics given by Symantec, around 5,000 websites have become the target of formjacking attacks.
4. **Inefficient cryptographic mechanisms**—Cryptographic mechanisms are crucial not only for data in transmission, but also for data

stored over the smart card or remote storage servers. Any vulnerability accompanied by these mechanisms can lead to the unauthorized manipulation of the data, which cannot be detected by the underlying system.

5. **Poor data segmentation**—Lack of appropriate data segmentation can lead to loss of congruence and uniformity in data.

4.2.3 Availability Loss

A repeated number of unauthorized system-level requests can block the authorized users from PIN access. Damage of hardware components, including the smart cards, readers, or remote servers, can also prevent users from accessing smart card–based services. Denial of service (DoS) attacks [14–19] also prevent availability of the data and services by creating situations such as infrastructure failure, which includes failure of storage devices, virtual servers performing transaction-related operations, communication channels, and so forth. Absence of sufficient backup and recovery mechanisms make the problem more severe. Infrastructure overloading also reflects the problem of data unavailability. Data inconsistencies can lead to changes in data format that cannot be quickly transformed into the required format and, thus, can lead to data unavailability.

4.2.4 Other Concerns

Other than the security threats and attacks discussed earlier, some factors exist that can affect the overall security of the data in the smart card–based application environment. These are as follows:

1. **Poor configuration management**—Lack of efficient data protection mechanisms may lead to failure to restrict the type of machine that can connect to the remote smart card–based application using a network, which can make the data associated with the application vulnerable to breach of confidentiality [20].

2. **Outdated policies**—Security policies play a major role in securing the data and governing the overall system. However, outdated polices can have a significant negative impact on the security of the data [21].

4.3 COUNTERMEASURES

Smart card–based applications involve many user interactions, which make users increasingly dependent on the cards. Therefore, it is vital to ensure secrecy and privacy of the security-intensive or sensitive data associated with the underlying systems or users. Securing the data involves secure management of the data storage (security-intensive information including PINs, passwords, etc.), secure transmission and distribution of the data over communication channels (cryptographic keys), and so forth. Securing the data storage can be associated with host-based security, which involves ensuring security of the memory cards or securing the remote storage servers from any kind of intrusions. The other aspect is card-based security, which involves a microprocessor card executing security algorithms and access control mechanisms to ensure authorized access and manipulations over the data. A simple model that covers all the aspects of data security is summarized in Table 4.1. Appropriate countermeasures for data-level security attacks are shown in Figure 4.2.

To achieve data confidentiality, improved cryptographic mechanisms can be used, including Data Encryption Standard (DES) [22], Triple DES, Rivest-Shamir-Adleman (RSA) Algorithm, International Data Encryption Algorithm (IDEA), Digital Signature Algorithm (DSA), elliptic curve cryptography (ECC), and hash-based algorithms. For data stored in the databases, privacy-preserving machine learning algorithms can be used [23]. Data masking techniques can also be used that involve creation and storage of the structurally similar but obfuscated data to prevent unauthorized access of original data. Communication channels must be secured for data transfer in a contactless card because they are vulnerable to interception.

TABLE 4.1   Data security model

TOOL CATEGORY	TOOL EXAMPLE
System analysis	Type of data, users, mode of communication, and data transmission
Risk analysis	Impact of loss of data
Threat analysis	Internal or external
System deployment	Security steps
Run-time testing	Security attack on the running system, finding loopholes
Fixing	Patches, re-deployment
Auditing and logging	Regular security monitoring, system checks, fine-tuning

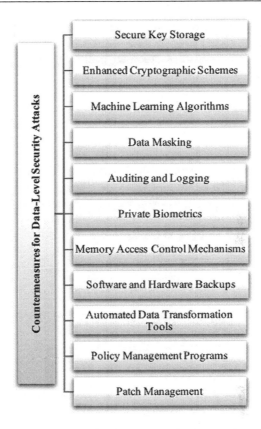

FIGURE 4.2   Countermeasures for data-level security attacks.

Swathi et al. [24] proposed an ATM security system that involves use of user-defined PIN and Global System for Mobile Communications (GSM). The security PIN is generated by the user, which is made available to the ATM machine through a subscriber identity module (SIM) present in the user's mobile phone.

To ensure data integrity, electronic cryptography techniques can be used that involve assignment of a unique identity to the data, such as a fingerprint. Whenever unauthorized manipulations or tampering of the data is occurring, the associated fingerprint flags the same, which preserves the characteristics of the underlying transaction. Auditing and logging mechanisms can be deployed to examine and record the data associated with the transactions in order to confirm their compliance with the already defined policies and procedures.

Use of private biometrics involves encrypted copy of the biometric information belonging to an individual being stored with the original copy in the storage databases. In later stages, the user is authenticated by comparing the input presented by the user with the already stored encrypted copy. It ensures that the original identifiers cannot be leaked or manipulated. Enhanced memory access control–based techniques can be employed for ensuring secure operating system support in case of smart cards capable of providing multiple applications.

To prevent DoS attacks from ceasing the operations of security application software, software backup mechanisms can be used. In case of situations involving attacks on the hardware to damage it, hardware backup systems can be deployed. Automated failover can be used to enable these hardware and software backup systems to ensure redundancy in case the main systems go down. To prevent availability loss due to infrastructure overloading, data infrastructure should be built with consideration for the goal of stability. To prevent data inconsistency, automated data transformation tools must be used that can ensure required transformation of data from one format to another while the data are in transit.

Robust policy management programs can be implemented to ensure periodic updating of the security policies. Guccione et al. [25] discussed the concept of domain trust evaluation and domain policy management functions in smart card–based systems for achieving effective control of security policy enforcement on smart card devices. Similarly, patch management programs implement software fixes in order to fill the existing loop holes and to connect hardware to the communication network involving transmission of data [26].

4.4 CONCLUSION

In this chapter, we outlined various security threats and attacks associated with data in smart card–based systems and applications. We classified them into those concerning confidentiality, integrity, and availability associated with the data. In addition, some additional security concerns, including management aspects of the system, were also discussed.

In the next chapter, we will discuss the role of remote user authentication mechanisms for ensuring legitimate resource access in smart card–based applications and possible attacks over the same, along with suitable countermeasures.

REFERENCES

1. Smart Card Basics. (2010). Smart card security. Retrieved from http://www.smartcardbasics.com/smart-card-security.html
2. Ward, B. (2015). Man versus machine: Can computers crack cryptography? Retrieved from https://epublications.regis.edu/cgi/viewcontent.cgi?article=1657&context=theses
3. Mayes, K. E., Markantonakis, K., Francis, L., & Hancke, G. P. (2010). NFC security threats. *Smart Card Technology International Magazine*, 42–47.
4. Kumari, S., & Khan, M. K. (2014). Cryptanalysis and improvement of "a robust smart-card-based remote user password authentication scheme." *International Journal of Communication Systems*, 27(12), 3939–3955.
5. Fledel, D., & Wool, A. (2018, August). Sliding-window correlation attacks against encryption devices with an unstable clock. In *International Conference on Selected Areas in Cryptography* (pp. 193–215). Cham, Switzerland: Springer.
6. Guo, C., Chang, C. C., & Chang, S. C. (2018). A secure and efficient mutual authentication and key agreement protocol with smart cards for wireless communications. *IJ Network Security*, 20(2), 323–331.
7. Markantonakis, K., & Main, D. (2017). Smart cards for banking and finance. In *Smart cards, tokens, security and applications* (pp. 129–153). Springer, Cham.
8. Pelletier, M. P., Trépanier, M., & Morency, C. (2011). Smart card data use in public transit: A literature review. *Transportation Research Part C: Emerging Technologies*, 19(4), 557–568.
9. Tandon, D., & Parimal, P. (2018). A case study on security recommendations for a global organization. *Journal of Computer and Communications*, 6(3), 128.
10. King, D. W., Schwarz, A., & Hunter, S. J. (2015). U.S. Patent No. 9,002,723. Washington, DC: U.S. Patent and Trademark Office.
11. Colorossi, J. L. (2015). Cyber security. In *Security supervision and management* (pp. 501–525). Waltham, MA: Butterworth-Heinemann.
12. Barbu, G., Thiebeauld, H., & Guerin, V. (2010, April). Attacks on Java Card 3.0 combining fault and logical attacks. In *International Conference on Smart Card Research and Advanced Applications* (pp. 148–163). Berlin, Germany: Springer.
13. Business Today. (2019). Formjacking: The new hack of cyber criminals to pilfer millions from consumers. https://www.businesstoday.in/technology/news/formjacking-the-new-hack-of-cyber-criminals-to-pilfer-millions-from-consumers/story/321031.html
14. Chhabra, M., Gupta, B., & Almomani, A. (2013). A novel solution to handle DDOS attack in MANET. *Journal of Information Security*, 4(3), 165.
15. Negi, P., Mishra, A., & Gupta, B. B. (2013). Enhanced CBF packet filtering method to detect DDoS attack in cloud computing environment. *International Journal of Computer Science Issues (IJCSI)*, 10(2 Part 1), 142.
16. Tripathi, S., Gupta, B., Almomani, A., Mishra, A., & Veluru, S. (2013). Hadoop based defense solution to handle distributed denial of service (DDOS) attacks. *Journal of Information Security*, 4(03), 150.

17. Srivastava, A., Gupta, B. B., Tyagi, A., Sharma, A., & Mishra, A. (2011, September). A recent survey on DDoS attacks and defense mechanisms. In *International Conference on Parallel Distributed Computing Technologies and Applications* (pp. 570–580). Berlin, Germany: Springer.

18. Gupta, B. B., & Badve, O. P. (2017). Taxonomy of DoS and DDoS attacks and desirable defense mechanism in a cloud computing environment. *Neural Computing and Applications, 28*(12), 3655–3682.

19. Alomari, E., Manickam, S., Gupta, B., Karuppayah, S., & Alfaris, R. (2012). Botnet-based distributed denial of service (DDoS) attacks on web servers: Classification and art. *International Journal of Computer Applications, 49*(7), 24–32.

20. Wentker, D. C., & Gungl, K. P. (2002). U.S. Patent No. 6,481,632. Washington, DC: U.S. Patent and Trademark Office.

21. Ahn, G. J. (2016). U.S. Patent No. 9,338,188. Washington, DC: U.S. Patent and Trademark Office.

22. Cachin, C., Sorniotti, M. V., & Weigold, T. (2016). Blockchain, cryptography, and consensus. Retrieved from https://cachin.com/cc/talks/20161004-blockchain-techtuesday-web.pdf

23. Lerman, L., Bontempi, G., & Markowitch, O. (2015). A machine learning approach against a masked AES. *Journal of Cryptographic Engineering, 5*(2), 123–139.

24. Swathi, H., Joshi, S., & Kumar, M. K. (2018, February). A novel ATM security system using a user defined personal identification number with the aid of GSM technology. In *2018 Second International Conference on Advances in Electronics, Computers and Communications (ICAECC)* (pp. 1–5). IEEE.

25. Guccione, L. J., Meyerstein, M. V., Cha, I., Schmidt, A., Leicher, A., & Shah, Y. C. (2016). U.S. Patent No. 9,363,676. Washington, DC: U.S. Patent and Trademark Office.

26. Baar, E. W., & Walters, P. L. (2018). U.S. Patent Application No. 15/875,537. Washington, DC: U.S. Patent and Trademark Office.

Remote User Authentication Mechanisms in Smart Card–Based Applications

5

5.1 INTRODUCTION

With the considerable progress in information technology (IT) and its applications, users can interact with intelligent services over the Internet by using different computing and communication devices. In this scenario, remote user authentication mechanisms provide accessibility of the resources, services, and applications to the users regardless of their physical location. They involve registration, identification, and verification of the user's credentials and unique identifying information provided by other communicating entities, such as servers. Using this information, these participating entities can authenticate and verify each other's legitimacy.

With the advent of the Internet of Things (IoT), the smart card–based application domain has expanded. Different authentication mechanisms have been adopted to ensure security of smart card–based systems [1]. These use single or multiple factors in combination, such as smart cards, passwords, biometric characteristics, and one-time password (OTP) for the authentication of the entities involved. Two main driving factors for such schemes are security and operational cost. However, most of them do not ensure complete security from all types of attacks. Increasing numbers of devices and users have made these schemes vulnerable to attacks, such as user impersonation, message forgery, denial of service (DoS) attacks, replay attacks, stolen smart card attacks, man-in-the-middle (MITM) attacks, and so on. These attacks can make it significantly difficult for a legitimate user to access a particular application or a service for some purpose. Moreover, designing a secure scheme for resource-constrained devices is challenging [2,3].

To prevent these attacks, a mature authentication scheme is required with enhanced security using stronger key agreement and improved computational efficiency. At the same time, it should support the dynamic profile of the users in different applications. In this chapter, we use some of the work done in this domain and propose an improved lightweight and multifactor authentication scheme based on elliptic curve cryptography (ECC) for the IoT environment [4–6].

The major contributions and highlights of the proposed work are as follows:

1. We discuss the flaws of existing multifactor remote authentication schemes for smart card–based applications, and to overcome the shortcomings of these schemes, we propose an improved remote authentication scheme.
2. The proposed scheme provides flexible four-factor authentication based on smart card, user's password, biometrics, and OTP, depending on the type of user and security level of the application, which makes it suitable for different smart card–based applications.
3. The proposed scheme is suitable for applications residing over multiple servers (i.e., multiserver environment) because the user is not required to maintain separate login credentials for each application.
4. The proposed scheme provides users the ability to freely choose and change the credentials.
5. We also discuss the execution of the proposed scheme on the Automated Validation of Internet Security Protocols and Applications (AVISPA) tool and the validation of the access control policy model on the Access Control Policy Testing (ACPT) tool.
6. The proposed scheme is resistant to a wide range of security attacks and provides enhanced functionality, which is demonstrated using detailed security and performance analysis. Formal security analysis using the method of contradiction is also presented.

The remainder of this chapter is structured as follows. In Section 5.2, we discuss the related work from the past. Section 5.3 describes the basics of ECC, collision-resistant one-way hash function, security and functional requirements that an authentication scheme must satisfy, and the threat assumptions used in the proposed scheme. In Section 5.4, we describe the system entities, system model, and detailed mathematical formulation of our scheme. Section 5.5 discusses the implementation details and results of the proposed scheme. Section 5.6 discusses the informal and formal security analysis of the proposed scheme, along with a comparison of the security features of our proposed scheme with some other related schemes. Section 5.7 provides comparative performance analysis of our scheme versus these related schemes, along with a description of the functional convenience from a user's perspective. Finally, Section 5.8 concludes the chapter and discusses some future work.

5.2 RELATED WORK

In 1981, Leslie Lamport was the first to propose a mechanism for authenticating a remote user based on password [7]. However, this scheme was proven to be susceptible to impersonation and replay attacks [8]. Since then, a number of authentication schemes with elevated security levels and performance efficiency, and based on different cryptographic mechanisms, have been proposed. Table 5.1 summarizes these schemes based on different cryptographic models.

TABLE 5.1 Authentication schemes based on different cryptographic models

TYPE OF SCHEMES	DESCRIPTION
Rivest–Shamir–Adleman (RSA)–based schemes [9]	Security relies on the problem of factoring large prime numbers.
Schemes based on hash functions [10]	Provide security to stored passwords as hash functions are infeasible to be inversed.
Schemes based on ElGamal model [11]	Provide enhanced security that depends on the difficulty of computing discrete logarithm over finite fields.
Elliptic curve cryptography (ECC)–based schemes [12]	Provide enhanced security with reduced key sizes based on difficulty of solving discrete logarithm problem.
One-time password (OTP)–based schemes [13]	Security relies on the problem of factoring large prime numbers.
Biometrics-based schemes [14]	Make use of biological characteristics of the user for identification and authentication and prevent forgery attacks.

Conventional two-factor authentication schemes involved the use of identity along with passwords and smart cards by the users to gain access to services of a remote server [15–17]. In most of the schemes, the received user credentials were matched with the ones already stored in the server's database. However, passwords were usually stored in the plain text form and were susceptible to exposure to unauthorized entities. To prevent this, schemes were proposed that involved passwords stored in encrypted form. Hash-based schemes were developed that involved applying a one-way hash function over the credentials in a secure manner, and those values were stored in the verifier table for future reference and verification [18]. However, many two-factor authentication schemes were still susceptible to impersonation attacks.

Later, three-factor authentication schemes [19–23] were developed that provided authentication based on biometrics of the user along with the passwords and smart cards. These techniques resolved the problem of impersonation attacks because the biometrics of a user are almost impossible to be forged. Mutlugun and Sogukpinar [23] proposed an idea of multilevel authentication using biometrics and passwords. It is based on Rivest–Shamir–Adleman (RSA) cryptosystem having high computational cost and large size keys. The scheme used the concept of policy server to decide on the authentication level for the user. Moon, Lee, Jung, and Won [24] proposed a biometric scheme based on ECC that could withstand user impersonation and insider and outsider attacks and could support perfect forward secrecy. However, a major shortcoming of these schemes is that they operate in an environment in which applications are running over the same server. To overcome this, multiserver authentication schemes [25–28] were developed. Recently, Yoon and Yoo [25] and Bae and Kwak [29] proposed schemes for the multiserver IoT environment. However, these schemes do not support flexible multilevel authentication. The scheme proposed in this chapter takes into account all of the previously mentioned drawbacks to overcome these issues.

5.3 PRELIMINARIES

This section elaborates the elementary ideas of ECC along with the functional and security requirements that a pertinent smart card–based remote authentication scheme should satisfy. We also discuss the threat model used in the proposed scheme to analyze its security.

5.3.1 Elliptic Curve Cryptography (ECC)

Miller [30] and Koblitz [31] independently suggested the use of an elliptic curve cryptosystem as a public key cryptosystem in 1985. It is often used in various authentication schemes to provide enhanced security along with performance efficiency with reduced parameter sizes, such as keys. Figures 5.1 and 5.2 show the comparison of the time taken by ECC and RSA to generate keys of different sizes. With keys of smaller size consuming less time for generation, ECC provides identical security as RSA, similar to other asymmetric key algorithms.

A nonsingular elliptic curve $E_p(u, v)$ over a finite prime field F_p, where p is a large prime number, is a set of solutions (x, y) lying on the curve and is defined by the Weierstrass equation [32], as given in Equation (5.1) below:

$$y^2 = x^3 + ux + v \left(\mathrm{mod}\, p \right) \tag{5.1}$$

where $(u, v) \in Z_p^*$ define the curve and satisfy the condition given in Equation (5.2) below:

$$4u^3 + 27v^2 \neq 0 \left(\mathrm{mod}\, p \right) \tag{5.2}$$

The identity element o lying on the curve is termed as the 'Point at Infinity'. Point addition and point multiplication, which is repeated point addition,

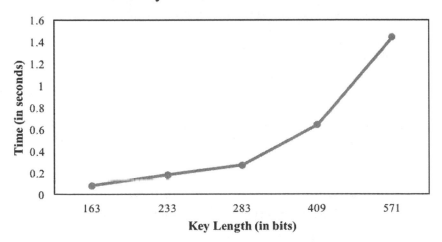

FIGURE 5.1   Elliptic Curve Cryptography (ECC) key generation performance.

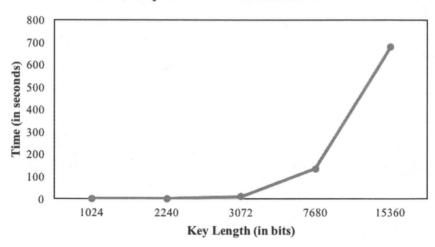

FIGURE 5.2   Rivest–Shamir–Adleman (RSA) key generation performance.

are the two elementary operations. If S is a point over the elliptic curve $E_p(u, v)$ and m is an integer, then point multiplication can be defined as given in Equation (5.3) below:

$$mS = S + S + \ldots \; S \, (m \text{ times})\qquad\qquad(5.3)$$

The hardness of solving the following two problems ensures the security of ECC [33]:

1. **Problem 1:** Elliptic Curve Discrete Logarithmic Problem (ECDLP)—*If S_1 and S_2 are two points over an elliptic curve $E_p(u, v)$, then it is computationally difficult to find an integer m in polynomial time such that $S_1 = mS_2$.*
2. **Problem 2:** Elliptic Curve Computational Diffie-Hellman Problem (ECCDH)—*If S_1, mS_1, and zS_1 are three points over an elliptic curve $E_p(u, v)$, then it is computationally difficult to find mzS_1 in polynomial time.*

5.3.2 Collision-Resistant One-Way Hash Function

Definition 1: A secure collision-resistant one-way hash function h(): $\{0, 1\}^* \rightarrow \{0, 1\}^n$ is defined as follows [27]: *It is a deterministic cryptographic algorithm* *that accepts a binary string x of unspecified length as input and generates a binary string of specified-length n as output.* Let $Adv_A^{HASH}(t)$ denote the advantage of an adversary A in determining the collision between hashed values of two different inputs. Then it can be defined by Equation (5.4), given below:

$$Adv_A^{HASH}(t) = Pr[(x, x') \in_R A : x \neq x' \text{ and } h(x) = h(x')] \tag{5.4}$$

where $Pr[E]$ denotes the probability of occurrence of an arbitrary event E, and x and x' are randomly selected by the probabilistic adversary A with running time t. A hash function $h()$ is termed as collision-resistant if $Adv_A^{HASH}(t) \leq \in_1$ for any sufficiently smaller $\in_1 > 0$.

5.3.3 Functional and Security Requirements

A pertinent mutual authentication scheme based on smart cards should satisfy the following functional and security requirements:

1. It should withstand various security attacks, including replay attacks, password guessing attacks, stolen smart card attacks, and impersonation attacks.
2. It should preserve user anonymity. In other words, the user's identity should not be revealed while the user is trying to log in or during the authentication phase.
3. It should provide user untraceability.
4. It should satisfy forward secrecy property.
5. The user must be capable of choosing his or her identity and password freely.
6. The user must be capable of updating his or her password freely.
7. It should support user eviction.
8. Computational and communication overheads should be low considering the resource-constrained environment.

5.3.4 Threat Assumptions

While developing the threat assumptions for our scheme according to the capabilities of the adversary A, we have considered the adversarial or threat model proposed by Danny Dolev and Andrew Yao [34] and the possibility of side-channel attacks [35]. These assumptions are given as follows:

1. An adversary A can be an intruder, a registered server, or a registered or false user of the underlying system.

2. An adversary A can capture messages being transmitted over a public communication channel between the two communicating parties (i.e., the user and the server in the current case).
3. An adversary A can reroute, recast, delete, or replay the captured message.
4. An adversary A can introduce a new message in the communication channel.
5. Power analysis attacks can be conducted to retrieve the sensitive information from the smart card that involve observing and analyzing power consumption of the card.

5.4 PROPOSED MODEL

In this section, we discuss our proposed remote user authentication scheme in detail, including the system entities, system model showing interaction among the system entities, and cryptographic formulation of the scheme.

5.4.1 System Entities

The following system entities are involved in our proposed scheme:

1. User (U_i)—A user is a person who is issued a smart card upon successful registration by authentication server to access the remote application. One access request can be made at a time. For each access request, the user enters the required credentials (i.e., username, password, fingerprints, or OTP). Access permission is given depending on the type of user and security level of the application. User can also request authentication server for change of credentials.
2. Smart Card (SC_i)—Smart card is user's possession with the help of which user can access the remote application. Some parameters are stored over the smart card for local computations. It supports access to multiple applications based on the security level assigned to these applications.
3. IoT Application Server (IS_j)—IoT application server is responsible for hosting the smart card–based application that can be remotely accessed. IoT server also needs to be successfully registered by the authentication server to host a particular application and needs to be authenticated in order to provide service to the remote user.

4. Authentication Server (*AS*)—The authentication server is a trusted entity responsible for issuing the smart card to the user and registration of IoT server. It also authenticates the user and the IoT server for establishment of secure communication between them. It can also deny user's access to the remote application and also provides facility to the user for changing the credentials.

5. Management Server (*MS*)—The management server is responsible for deciding the authentication or security level upon user's request. Authentication level depends on the type of user and security requirement of the application.

6. Client Application—The client application is an application running over the user's machine to provide accessibility of the remote application.

5.4.2 System Model

The proposed model is shown in Figure 5.3. It initially involves registration of the user and the IoT application server by the authentication server based on the identifying information provided by both. Upon successful registration, a smart card is issued to the user with secret parameters stored over it, including anonymous information of the user. The application server gets server-related information as registration response. The client application sends its application tag to the smart card, which in turn sends it along with the user's anonymous information to the management server to get the required authentication level as a response.

When the card comes in contact with or in close proximity to the card reader, the user enters the required credentials. The reader sends these credentials along with other parameters in the form of a login request to the IoT application server, which in turn appends its own information to the login request and sends the same to the authentication server requesting for authentication. The authentication server performs necessary operations and sends the authentication response along with the session key to the application server, which then forwards the necessary information to the smart card. It also sets the status-bit corresponding to the user to 1 in order to deny multiple login requests. The smart card computes the session key and sends the authentication declaration used in the login operation to the client application. The client application sends the authentication declaration to the authentication server via the application server for verification. Upon successful verification of the declaration, the authentication server sends a success message to the application server, which then decides whether or not the user with a particular identity is

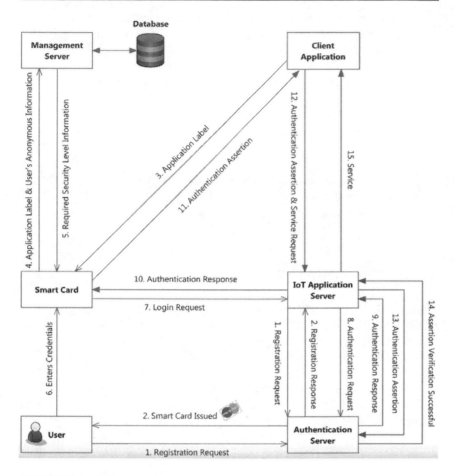

FIGURE 5.3   System model.

eligible to access the application. The user gets the required service from the application server through the client application.

5.4.3 System Working

In this subsection, we present the cryptographic details of the steps involved in our authentication scheme. It consists of eight phases in total, with six involved in the user authentication and the remaining two involving change of user's credentials and user eviction. Figure 5.4 shows the flowchart depicting the working of the proposed scheme.

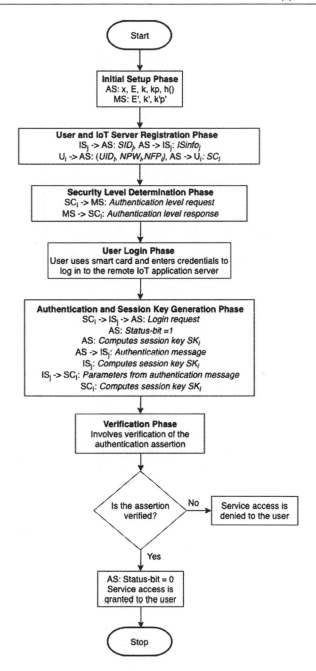

FIGURE 5.4   Working flowchart of the proposed scheme. See Table 5.2 for terms.

TABLE 5.2   Notations used

TERM	DESCRIPTION
X	Secret symmetric key of authentication scheme (AS)
E, F_p, G, P	Elliptic curve, field, additive group, generator of AS
$E', F'_{p'}, G', P'$	Elliptic curve, field, additive group, generator of management server (MS)
p, n, p', n'	Prime numbers
k, kP	Private and public keys of AS
$k', k'P'$	Private and public keys of MS
SK_i	Session key
$Z_n^*, Z_{n'}^*$	Nonzero integers modulo the prime number n and n'
$h()$	Hash function
SID_j	IoT application server identity
$ISinfo_j$	IoT server information
UID_i	User identity
PW_i	User password
r_i	Random number chosen by the user
FP_i	User fingerprint
a_i	Password verifier
$Uinfo_i$	User anonymous information
L	Application tag
T	Timestamp
SL	Security level
V	Validity period of the authentication declaration

The notations used while formulating the scheme are listed in Table 5.2.

The working phases are explained in detail as follows:

1. Initial Setup Phase—This phase involves generation of initial system parameters that are maintained by the authentication server *AS* and the management server *MS* for future computations.
    - *AS:*
        a. maintains a secret key x.
        b. considers an elliptic curve E over the finite field F_p and selects a generator P of an additive group G of order n (p and n are large prime numbers).
        c. selects a private key $k \in Z_n^*$. From this private key, it computes public key $= kP$.

    d. chooses a secure one-way hash function $h()$: $\{0, 1\}^* \rightarrow$ $\{0, 1\}^n$ that is collision resistant (based on MD5 or SHA-1) with fixed output.

    e. publishes the parameters $\{E(F_p), G, n, P, h()\}$.

- *MS:*
  a. considers an elliptic curve E' over the finite field $F'_{p'}$ and selects a generator P' of an additive group G' of order n' (p' and n' are large prime numbers).
  b. selects a private key $k' \in Z_{n'}^*$. From this private key, it computes public key $= k'P'$.
  c. publishes the parameters $\{E'(F'_{p'}), G', n', P'\}$.

2. User and IoT Server Registration Phase—During the registration phase, the user U_i and the IoT application server IS_j request the authentication server AS for registration. In return, user U_i receives a smart card SC_i from the authentication server, and the IoT server IS_j gets secret identifying information for verification phase. It is assumed that the IoT server and the authentication server communicate across a secure channel.

- IS_j sends its identity SID_j to AS as registration request.
- *AS:*
  a. computes $ISinfo_j = h(SID_j \| x)$.
  b. returns $ISinfo_j$ as registration response to IS_j.

- U_i:
  a. chooses a username UID_i and a password PW_i along with a random number $r_i \in Z_n^*$.
  b. computes $NPW_i = h(r_i \| PW_i)$.
  c. submits his fingerprints FP_i to the sensor S.
  d. computes $NFP_i = h(r_i \| FP_i)$.
  e. sends registration request (UID_i, NPW_i, NFP_i) to AS through a secure channel.

- *AS:*
  a. calculates password verifier $a_i = E_x(UID_i \| NPW_i \| NFP_i)$.
  b. calculates $Uinfo_i = h(UID_i \| x)$.
  c. stores $\{Uinfo_i, a_i, kP, k'P', h()\}$ on the smart card SC_i.
  d. stores $\{UID_i, a_i\}$ in the verification table maintained by it [Table 5.3].
  e. provides a smart card SC_i to U_i.

- User U_i stores the random number r_i into the smart card SC_i.

TABLE 5.3   The verification table

USER ID	PASSWORD VERIFIER	STATUS-BIT
UID_1	a_1	0/1
UID_2	a_2	0/1
...	...	...

3. Security Level Determination Phase—In this phase, management server MS collects the application tag L and user's anonymous information $Uinfo_i$ from the smart card SC_i and decides which security level is applicable for the user U_i for that particular application.

   - Client application sends application tag L to the smart card SC_i.
   - SC_i:
     a. generates a nonce s_1.
     b. computes $M_0' = s_1 P'$, $M_0 = (Uinfo_i \parallel L \parallel s_1) + s_1 k'P'$.
     c. sends an authentication level request (M_0', M_0) to management server MS.

   - MS:
     a. gets $Uinfo_i$, L, and s_1 by computing:

     $$M_0 - k'M_0' = (Uinfo_i \parallel L \parallel s_1) + s_1 k'P' - s_1 k'P' = (Uinfo_i \parallel L \parallel s_1).$$

     b. decides on security level SL, timestamp T, and validity period V using $Uinfo_i$ and L.
     c. chooses a random number m and computes $M_1' = mP'$, $M_1 = (SL \parallel T \parallel V) + ms_1 P'$.
     d. sends authentication level response (M_1', M_1) to the smart card SC_i.

   - SC_i:
     a. calculates $M_1 - s_1 M_1'$ and gets the required details SL, T, and V.
     b. accepts the security level SL (SL = 1 - Card only, SL = 2 - Password, SL = 3 - Fingerprint, SL = 4 - OTP, SL = 5 - Password and Fingerprint, SL = 6 - Password and OTP, SL = 7 - Password, Fingerprint, and OTP).

4. User Login Phase—This phase involves the user U_i entering the credentials.
   - Smart card SC_i is inserted in the reader or comes in proximity with the reader, and user U_i enters the username UID_i', password PW_i', and fingerprint FP_i' in the fingerprint sensor S.

5. Authentication and Session Key Generation Phase—During this phase, the authentication server AS authenticates the user U_i as a legitimate user and the IoT server IS_j. It also generates a session key SK_i.

- SC_i calculates the following:
    a. If $SL = 2 \Rightarrow NPW_i' = h(r_i \parallel PW_i')$.
    b. If $SL = 3 \Rightarrow NFP_i' = h(r_i \parallel FP_i')$.
    c. If $SL = 4 \Rightarrow$ asks for OTP.
    d. If $SL = 5 \Rightarrow$ both steps a) and b).
    e. If $SL = 6 \Rightarrow$ both steps a) and c).
    f. If $SL = 7 \Rightarrow$ steps a), b), and c).

- SC_i will do the following:
    a. Generates two random numbers s_2 and b
    b. Calculates $M_2' = bP$, $M_2 = (UID_i' \parallel a_i \parallel s_2 \parallel L \parallel SL \parallel T \parallel V \parallel NPW_i' \parallel NFP_i' \parallel OTP) + bkP$
    c. Sends a login request message (M_2', M_2) to the IoT application server IS_j

- On receiving the login request message from the user, IS_j does the following:
    a. Chooses a random number l
    b. Calculates $B_j = ISinfo_j \oplus l$ and $C_j = h(lkP \parallel l)$
    c. Sends $(M_2', M_2, SID_j', B_j, C_j)$ to AS

- AS:
    a. computes $M_2 - kM_2'$ to get the required details.
    b. checks whether $T <$ current time $< T+V$.
    c. computes $ISinfo_j'$ using SID_j' and x.

    $$ISinfo_j' = h(SID_j' \parallel x)$$

    d. computes l' using $ISinfo_j'$ and B_j.

    $$l' = ISinfo_j' \oplus B_j$$

    e. computes C_j' using l', k, and P, and checks if $C_j' = C_j$. If matched, implies it is a valid IoT server.
    f. computes $D_x(a_i) = (UID_i \parallel NPW_i \parallel NFP_i)$ using secret key x.
    g. checks weather $UID_i' = UID_i$.
    h. if matched, finds its entry in the verification table. If present, sets status-bit $= 1$ and tests SL:
        i. If $SL = 1 \Rightarrow$ does not check anything.
        ii. If $SL = 2 \Rightarrow$ checks if $NPW' = NPW$.

      iii.   If $SL = 3 \Rightarrow$ checks if $NFP' = NFP$.

      iv.   If $SL = 4 \Rightarrow$ checks OTP.

      v.   If $SL = 5 \Rightarrow$ performs steps II and III.

      vi.   If $SL = 6 \Rightarrow$ performs steps II and IV.

      vii.   If $SL = 7 \Rightarrow$ performs steps II, III, and IV.

  i. prepares:

      i. $N = E_x(UID_i \parallel L \parallel T \parallel V)$.

      ii. $D_j = s_2 \oplus d \oplus h(SID_j \oplus l')$, where d is a random number chosen by AS.

      iii. $E_j = l' \oplus d \oplus h(a_i)$.

      iv. $SK_i = h(s_2 \oplus l' \oplus d)$.

      v. $M_3' = dP$, $M_3 = (N \parallel s_2 \parallel E_j) + da_iP$.

      vi.   sends authentication message (M_3, M_3', D_j, E_j) to IS_j.

- IS_j:
  a. computes $s_2 \oplus d = D_j \oplus h(SID_j \oplus l)$.
  b. computes $SK_i = h(s_2 \oplus l \oplus d)$.
  c. sends (M_3, M_3', E_j) to SC_i.

- SC_i:
  a. retrieves N and s_2 from $M_3 - a_iM_3'$.
  b. checks whether s_2 is same as previously sent one.
  c. computes $l \oplus d = E_j \oplus h(a_i)$.
  d. computes $SK_i = h(s_2 \oplus l \oplus d)$.
  e. sends $UID_i' \parallel N$ to client application.

6. Verification Phase—In this phase, the authentication declaration sent by client application to the authentication server AS via IoT application server IS_j is verified depending on which user gets the service.
   - Client application sends $(L \parallel UID_i' \parallel N \parallel SK_i)$ as declaration to IS_j.
   - IS_j sends this declaration to AS through a secure channel for verification.
   - AS:
     a. computes $D_x(N) = UID_i \parallel L \parallel T \parallel V$.
     b. compares decrypted UID_i value with plain UID_i' and decrypted L value with plain L.
     c. checks whether $T <$ current time $< T + V$.
     d. checks SK_i.

- After verification, AS returns success message to IS_j and sets status-bit = 0.
- IS_j checks whether U_i having UID_i is authorized for application tag L.

7. Password Change Phase—This phase involves the user making a password change request to the authentication server.
   - User U_i inserts the smart card in the reader or comes in proximity to the reader and enters UID_i', FP_i', and PW_i'.
   - SC_i computes NPW_i', NFP_i' and sends (UID_i', NPW_i', NFP_i') to AS.
   - AS checks for UID_i' in its verification table. If found, computes a_i' to check if $a_i' = a_i$.
   - If matched, U_i enters new password, and new value of a_i is calculated again by AS and is replaced on SC_i and in the verification table as well.

8. User Dismissal Phase—In case a user U_i is dismissed by authentication server AS, AS deletes the entry $\{UID_i, a_i\}$ from its verifier table and U_i cannot use UID_i to log in since its entry is not present in the verification table.

5.5 EXPERIMENTS AND RESULTS

In this section, we discuss the experimental results of the proposed model.

5.5.1 Prerequisites for the Experiments

AVISPA. AVISPA stands for Automated Validation of Internet Security Protocols and Applications [36]. It is a push-button tool that is used for the analysis of Internet-based security protocols. It provides a modular, role-based, and expressive formal language, called High-Level Protocol Specification Language (HLPSL), for the specification of protocols and the security properties associated with them. It also integrates different back-ends, including On-the-Fly Model-Checker (OFMC), Satisfiability (SAT)-Based Model Checker (SATMC), Constrained Logic–Based Attack Searcher (CL-AtSe), and Tree Automata based on Automatic Approximations for the Analysis of Security Protocols (TA4SP) analyzer, that perform a variety of automatic analysis over the protocols. AVISPA translates the user-defined security problem into an Intermediate Format (IF), which describes an infinite-state transition system responsive to the formal analysis. The IF specifications are provided as input to the back-ends that implement the attack analysis over the problem in hand.

SPAN. SPAN stands for Security Protocol Animator [36]. It is an animator for HLPSL-based specifications. It facilitates interactive creation of message sequence charts (MSC) of the protocol under execution and displays them using its local graphical user interface (GUI). The MSC can be generated for both the normal mode of functionality and intruder mode. Multiple sessions can be displayed based on the information given in the roles of the entities involved. Other than MSC, SPAN also shows the incoming as well as the past events. It checks for the values of all the variables that can be used by the user for monitoring each role.

ACPT. The Access Control Policy Testing (ACPT) tool was developed by the National Institute of Standards and Technology–Computer Science Division (NIST-CSD) as a prototype system for policy specification, implementation, and verification [37]. It is a Java-based tool that provides GUI templates for defining access control policies and a Symbolic Model Verification (SMV) model checker for checking access control policy models. It also provides NIST's Automated Combinatorial Testing for Software (ACTS) tool for generating test suite. Once the user-defined access control model is verified, the output is generated in eXtensible Access Control Markup Language (XACML) format.

5.5.2 Modeling of the Authentication Mechanism in AVISPA-SPAN

As stated earlier, the remote user authentication mechanism for smart card–based applications proposed in this dissertation work is modeled using the AVISPA tool in HLPSL language, which verifies the security properties associated with the mechanism, including the messages being transmitted and authentication of the entities involved. The model consists of the following modules:

1. Basic Roles—Basic roles correspond to the entities involved in our proposed mechanism including user, authentication server, management server, and IoT application server, which are denoted as UI, AS, MS, and IOT. An example of basic role declaration for management server is given below:

   ```
   %% Management server role management(MS, UI: agent,
   RCV, SND: channel(dy))played_by UI def=

   local State: nat,
   ```

```
S1, P, UiD, X, L, K, M, Q, SL, T, V: text,

Hash: function init State := 0 transition 1. State =
0 /\ RCV(S1'.P.Hash(UiD.X').L.S1'.S1'.K.P) =|>
State' := 1 /\ M' := new() /\ SND(M'.Q.SL.T.V.M'.
S1.Q) end role
```

2. Transitions—"State" is used to model the behavior of the system. In every state, variables belonging to a particular role hold some values, and when these values change, the state of the system also changes, which in turn is known as state transition.

3. Composed Roles—A composed role is a composition of basic roles interacting with each other. Composed roles do not contain any transitions but instantiate the basic roles and describe the session of the protocol. Description for the session in our mechanism is given as follows:

```
%% Session

role session(IOT, AS, UI, MS: agent, Xor : function,
KSAT, KSTC : (symmetric_key) set) def=

local SND, RCV: channel(dy) composition
application(IOT, AS, Xor, KSAT, SND, RCV) /\
authentication(IOT, AS, UI, Xor, KSAT, KSTC, RCV,
SND) /\ user(IOT, AS, UI, MS, Xor, KSTC, SND, RCV)
/\ management(MS, UI, RCV, SND) end role
```

4. Environment—Finally, the environment that is used for the execution of the protocol is defined, which contains the initial knowledge of the intruder along with the initial setting for the sessions. Description of environment in our proposed mechanism is given as follows:

```
%% Environment

role environment() def= local Ksat, Kstc:
(symmetric_key) set

const exor: function, subs, subs1, subs2: protocol_
id, as, iot, ui, ms: agent

intruder_knowledge = {as, iot, ui, ms} composition
session(iot, as, ui, ms, exor, Ksat, Kstc) end
role
```

TABLE 5.4   Initial parameter settings

PARAMETERS	ATTRIBUTES	ATTRIBUTE TYPE	ATTRIBUTE VALUES
Subject	Role	String	User, Administrator
Resource	S_L	Integer	0, 1, 2, 3, 4, 5, 6, 7
Action	SC, PW, OTP, FP, PIN	String	PROVIDED, NOT_PROVIDED
Environment	VALUES	String	VALID, INVALID

5.5.3 Policy Formulation in ACPT

In our proposed model, we use Attribute-Based Access Control (ABAC) to define the security policies. We have used the GUI provided by the ACPT tool to specify the properties associated with the policies. The initial parameter values for the proposed model are shown in Table 5.4. Two subjects have been considered for smart card–based applications: user and administrator. The user credentials that are used for controlling the access to the system services are smart card (SC), password (PW), fingerprint (FP), and OTP, which is received on the registered mobile number or email address. Similarly, the administrator who is responsible for managing the access control tasks provides the smart card SC and a security Personal Identification Number (PIN) to enter the system or the application. Different security levels denoted by S_L are defined ranging from integral values 0 to 7 with different credential requirements, as shown in Table 5.5. The application with S_L = 1 is least security sensitive, whereas the application with S_L = 7 deals with highly secured information. S_L = 0 is kept for identifying the administrator.

After defining the access control policies, XACML representation is created by mapping the attributes taken in those policies to the corresponding XACML attributes. Figure 5.5 shows a sample rule for the security policy of the proposed model in XACML format.

TABLE 5.5   Authenticator involved at each security level

PARAMETERS	ATTRIBUTES	ATTRIBUTE TYPE
0	PIN	Administrator
1	—	User
2	Password	
3	Fingerprint	
4	One-time password (OTP)	
5	Both password and fingerprint	
6	Both password and OTP	
7	Password, fingerprint, and OTP	

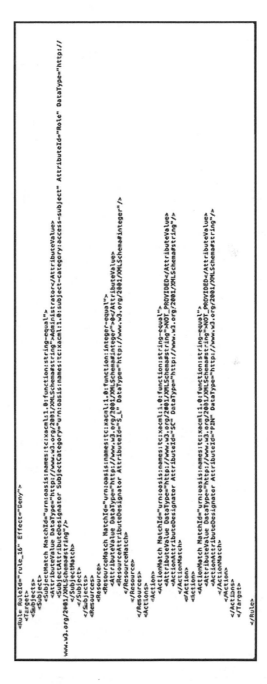

FIGURE 5.5   XACML representation of defined policies.

5.5.4 Results and Discussion

In this subsection, we present a discussion on the security policy verification of the proposed mechanism in the ACPT tool, including its static and dynamic verification. We also present simulation results on the AVISPA tool.

Policy Verification. Policy verification includes the following:

Static Verification or Property Verification—Static verification involves checking whether or not the properties of a policy are satisfied to ensure correct behavior of the policy. NuSMV is used for this purpose, which verifies a policy P against its properties p_i, where p_i is a logical formula to determine whether a particular state is reachable or not for a given set of constraints. NuSMV checks for any state violating the properties of a policy by reporting with counterexamples.

Dynamic Verification or Test Input Generation—In dynamic verification, correctness of policies in a system is verified based on the output of the test inputs, which is compared with the expected output. Thus, dynamic verification adds an additional level of confidence to the correctness of the policy by executing test inputs and acts as complimentary for static verification. These test inputs are based on both structural and combinatorial coverage that reduces the size of the test suite and, at the same time, provides sufficient level of confidence for policy correctness. Whereas the structural test input generation is called white-box testing, combinatorial test input generation is called black-box testing. Figure 5.6 shows the results of the verification of a proposed security policy model in ACPT. The results that are shown here cover three test cases out of a total of 16 test cases. Based on the access decisions of these results (i.e., Permit and Deny), we can compare them with the intended results (i.e., whether access should be granted or denied). Table 5.6 shows the execution time of static and dynamic verification for the proposed model.

Simulation Results. Figure 5.7 shows the MSC for our HLPSL specification, whereas Figure 5.8 and Figure 5.9 show the verification results obtained from OFMC and CL-AtSe back-ends in the AVISPA tool. From these results, it can be concluded that our proposed mechanism is safe against security attacks

TABLE 5.6   Running time for policy verification

VERIFICATION	RUNNING/ EXECUTION TIME
Static verification	203 ms
Dynamic verification	0.109 s

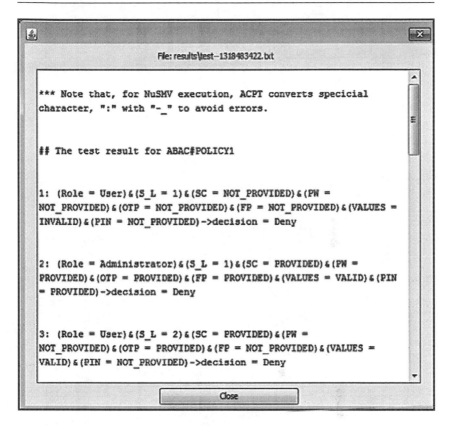

File: results\test–1318483422.txt

```
*** Note that, for NuSMV execution, ACPT converts specicial
character, ":" with "-_" to avoid errors.


## The test result for ABAC#POLICY1


1: (Role = User)&(S_L = 1)&(SC = NOT_PROVIDED)&(PW =
NOT_PROVIDED)&(OTP = NOT_PROVIDED)&(FP = NOT_PROVIDED)&(VALUES =
INVALID)&(PIN = NOT_PROVIDED)->decision = Deny


2: (Role = Administrator)&(S_L = 1)&(SC = PROVIDED)&(PW =
PROVIDED)&(OTP = PROVIDED)&(FP = PROVIDED)&(VALUES = VALID)&(PIN
= PROVIDED)->decision = Deny


3: (Role = User)&(S_L = 2)&(SC = PROVIDED)&(PW =
NOT_PROVIDED)&(OTP = PROVIDED)&(FP = NOT_PROVIDED)&(VALUES =
VALID)&(PIN = NOT_PROVIDED)->decision = Deny
```

Close

FIGURE 5.6   Policy verification results in ACPT.

and maintains the secrecy of the transmission and authentication of the communicating entities.

5.6 SECURITY ANALYSIS

In this section, we establish and prove that our proposed scheme preserves the security-related merits of existing schemes and can withstand several other possible types of attacks. The proposed scheme also prevents password guessing attacks and satisfies security properties such as user anonymity and multilevel authentication in a multiserver environment. The threat assumptions made in Section 5.3 are used for performing the informal and formal security analysis of the proposed scheme.

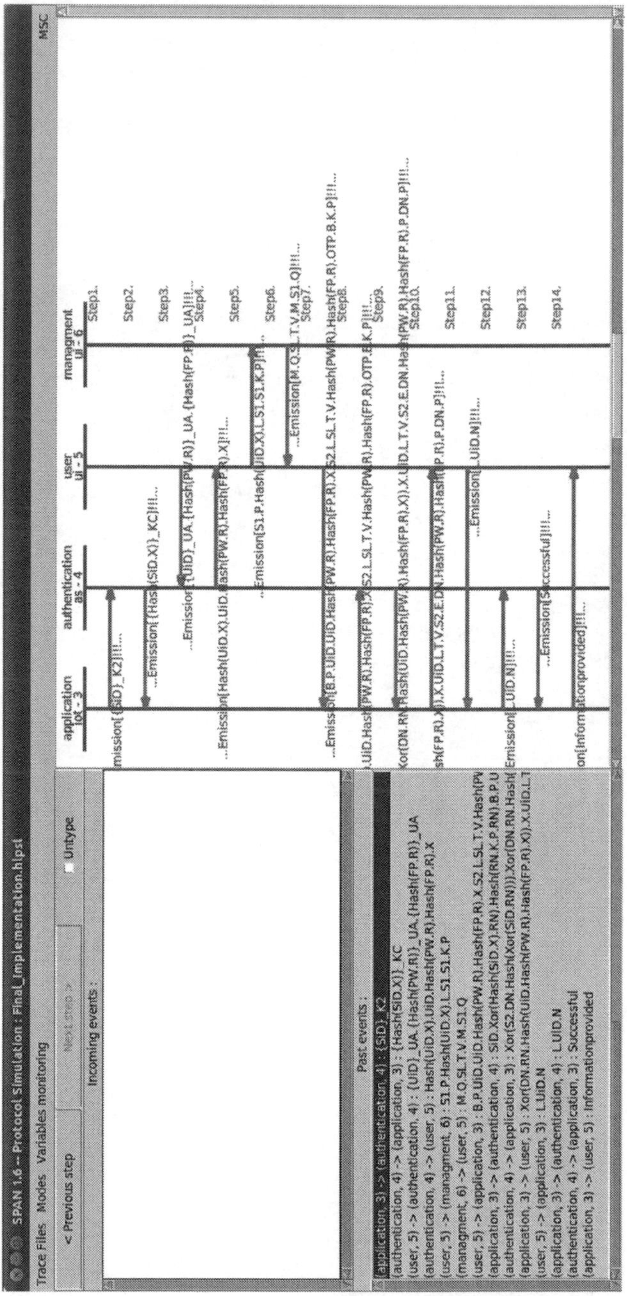

FIGURE 5.7 Message sequence chart (MSC) of the proposed mechanism in SPAN.

```
% OFMC
% Version of 2006/02/13
SUMMARY
 SAFE
DETAILS
 BOUNDED_NUMBER_OF_SESSIONS
PROTOCOL
 /home/span/span/testsuite/results/Final_Implementation.if
GOAL
 as_specified
BACKEND
 OFMC
COMMENTS
STATISTICS
 parseTime: 0.00s
 searchTime: 9.46s
 visitedNodes: 7137 nodes
 depth: 13 plies
```

FIGURE 5.8   Security verification with OFMC back-end.

```
SUMMARY
 SAFE

DETAILS
 BOUNDED_NUMBER_OF_SESSIONS
 TYPED_MODEL

PROTOCOL
 /home/span/span/testsuite/results/Final_Implementation.if

GOAL
 As Specified

BACKEND
 CL-AtSe

STATISTICS

 Analysed  : 7 states
 Reachable : 6 states
 Translation: 0.05 seconds
```

FIGURE 5.9   Security verification with CL-AtSe back-end.

5.6.1 Informal Security Analysis

Table 5.7 summarizes the various possible attack types that the proposed scheme can withstand and different security characteristics that it supports.

TABLE 5.7   Informal security analysis of the proposed scheme

ATTACK TYPE	DESCRIPTION
Stolen smart card attack	• $Uinfo_i$ does not reveal anything about the original identity of the user. • a_i is encrypted with the authentication server's private key and hence cannot be decrypted by the attacker without the key. • kP and $k'P'$ are public keys of the authentication and management server, respectively, and are already known to everyone. • $h()$ is a one-way function. • r_i cannot be used to log in in any case because username, biometrics, and one-time password (OTP) are also required for complete authentication at different security levels.
Insider attack	User password and fingerprints are not stored on the server in plain text form and are sent to the server only after performing hashing.
Password guessing attack	Attacker cannot verify whether the guessed password is correct because it is encrypted using authentication server's secret key x along with the fingerprints of the legitimate user, which cannot be forged, and these are stored on the smart card in the form of a_i.
Replay attack	Use of nonce (s_1, s_2, b, l) and timestamp T prevents replay attacks.
Stolen verifier attack	Attacker cannot infer anything from a_i without knowing the secret key of the authentication server.
Server spoofing attack	Identity of Internet of Things (IoT) server is verified by the authentication server and authentication server is assumed to be trusted.

(Continued)

TABLE 5.7 (Continued)   Informal security analysis of the proposed scheme

ATTACK TYPE	DESCRIPTION
Parallel session attack	Status-bit is set to 1 once a login request is received until the time of successful verification, and hence, another request made during the same interval is denied.
Modification attack	Data are transmitted in encrypted form.
Man-in-the-middle attack	• Not possible because of authentication. • Information is also transmitted in encoded form.
Denial of service (DoS) attack	Status-bit has been used to prevent DoS attacks that may be conducted due to multiple login requests.
Fake server attack	• Policy request can be opened by management server's private key k' only. • Login request can be opened by authentication server's private key k only.
Temporary information attack	Hash function $h()$ is used during the computations.
Privacy of fingerprint and password of the user	Stored on smart card in encoded form and not extracted anywhere in the plain text form.
Authentication	Both the user and the IoT application server are authenticated by the authentication server.
Impersonation attack	UID_i is not stored on the smart card, and login request to AS does not contain UID_i in plain text form.
Provide user the capability of freely choosing the username and the password	During the registration phase, user can freely choose the username and password.
Multilevel security	Different authenticators are used based on the type of user and the security level of the application to determine the authentication level.
Multifactor authentication	Flexible four-factor authentication based on card, password, fingerprint, and OTP has been used.
Secure server-side fingerprint verification	Fingerprints of the user are matched at the server side, thus preventing client-side verification attacks.

(Continued)

TABLE 5.7 (Continued)   Informal security analysis of the proposed scheme

ATTACK TYPE	DESCRIPTION
Forgery attacks	Attacker cannot generate messages on behalf of management and authentication server because of the unavailability of the keys.
Session key security	Session key is known to legitimate entities only because random numbers s_2, l, and d used to calculate the same are not known to adversary.
User untraceability	Each login request is independent from the previous one due to new random numbers chosen every time.
User anonymity	Plaintext UID_i is not used anywhere during the transmission; $Uinfo_i$ is computed by applying hash operation over UID_i and secret symmetric key of the authentication server.
Known-key secrecy	For every session, new random numbers are chosen to compute the session key. Thus, even if an attacker obtains the keys of older sessions, these cannot be used to derive session keys for future sessions.

5.6.2 Formal Security Analysis

To present the formal security analysis of our proposed scheme, we use the method of contradiction [38] under the generic group model of cryptography [39] to assert that our scheme can withstand an adversarial attack under an assumption that the adversary has access to the following two oracles:

1. **Oracle 1**—Considering hash value $y = h(x)$ for some input x, Oracle 1 will unconditionally regenerate the input x out of hash value y.
2. **Oracle 2**—Considering the generator P and the public key $kP \in E_q(a, b)$, Oracle 2 will unconditionally generate the private key k.

Theorem 5.1. *Our proposed scheme is secure from a polynomial-time adversary who tries to deduce the private key* k *of the authentication server* AS, *if one-way hash function* h() *behaves like an oracle, under the Elliptic Curve Discrete Logarithmic Problem (ECDLP).*

Proof of Theorem 5.1—To prove this theorem, we consider an adversary A having the ability to derive the private key k of the authentication server AS. The adversary A uses Oracle 1 and Oracle 2 to run the trial Algorithm 5.1

$ALGO1_{A,RAS}^{HASH,ECDLP}$ over the proposed remote authentication scheme (say RAS). The success probability for this trial is defined in Equation (5.5) as:

$$Success1 = \left| 2Pr[ALGO1_{A,RAS}^{HASH,ECDLP} = 1] - 1 \right| \tag{5.5}$$

where $Pr[X]$ denotes the probability of occurrence of an event X. The advantage function for the adversary A corresponding to this trial is defined in Equation (5.6) as:

$$Adv1(rt1, q_{O1}, q_{O2}) = \max_A \{Success1\} \tag{5.6}$$

where maximum $\max_A$ is taken over all the adversaries A with running time $rt1$. Here, q_{O1} and q_{O2} represent the number of queries made to Oracle 1 and Oracle 2, respectively. We claim that our scheme is provably secure against an adversary A for deriving the private key k of the authentication server AS, if $Adv1(rt1, q_{O1}, q_{O2}) \le \epsilon$, for any sufficiently smaller $\epsilon > 0$. If by executing the trial Algorithm 5.1 $ALGO1_{A,RAS}^{HASH,ECDLP}$, the adversary A has the ability to invert the one-way hash function $h()$ and solve ECDLP, then he or she can deduce the private key k of the authentication server AS and win the game. However, inversion of the hash function $h()$ is computationally infeasible, i.e., $Adv_A^{HASH}(t) \le \epsilon_1$ (Definition 1), for any sufficiently smaller $\epsilon_1 > 0$. Moreover, it is computationally infeasible to compute the discrete logarithm in elliptic curves due to difficulty of solving the same in polynomial time, as $Adv_{C,Eq(a,b)}^{ECDLP}(t) \le \epsilon_2$, for any sufficiently smaller $\epsilon_2 > 0$ (Problem 1). Hence, we have $Adv1(rt1, q_{O1}, q_{O2}) \le \epsilon$, since $Adv1(rt1, q_{O1}, q_{O2})$ depends on both the advantages $Adv_A^{HASH}(t)$ and $Adv_{C,Eq(a,b)}^{ECDLP}(t)$, for any sufficiently smaller $\epsilon > 0$. This proves that our proposed scheme is secure against an adversary A for deriving the private key k.

Algorithm 5.1 $ALGO1_{A,RAS}^{HASH,ECDLP}$

---

1. Attacker intercepts the message (M_2', M_2, SID_j', B_j, C_j) during the authentication phase, where $M_2' = bP$, $M_2 = (UID_i' \parallel a_i \parallel s_2 \parallel L \parallel SL \parallel T \parallel V \parallel NPW_i' \parallel NFP_i' \parallel OTP) + bkP$, $B_j = ISinfo_j \oplus I$, and $C_j = h(IkP \parallel I)$.
2. Attacker calls Oracle1 for input C_j to obtain the information IkP and I as ($IkP \parallel I$) ← Oracle1(C_j).
3. Attacker calls Oracle2 for input IkP to obtain the private key k as k' ← Oracle2(IkP).
4. Attacker computes $M_2 - k'M_2'$ and get the necessary details.
5. if $T <$ current time $< T+V$ then
6. Accepts k' as the correct private key of the authentication server AS.
7. return 1 or Success
8. else
9. return 0 or Failure
10. end if

Theorem 5.2. *Our proposed scheme is secure against p polynomial-time adversary who tries to deduce the session key* SK *used by authentication server, IoT application server, and user, if one-way hash function* h() *behaves like an oracle.*

Proof of Theorem 5.2—The proof of this theorem is similar to the one presented for Theorem 1. To prove this theorem, we consider an adversary A having an ability to extract the session key SK used by the authentication server, IoT application server, and user. The adversary A makes use of Oracle 1 to run the trial algorithm, say $ALGO2_{A,RAS}^{HASH}$, for the proposed remote authentication scheme RAS. The probability of success for this trail is given by Equation (5.7) as:

$$Success2 = \left| 2Pr[ALGO2_{A,RAS}^{HASH} = 1] - 1 \right| \tag{5.7}$$

where $Pr[X]$ denotes the probability of occurrence of an event X. The advantage function for the adversary A for this trial is defined by Equation (5.8) as:

$$Adv2(rt2, qO1) = \max A \{Success2\} \tag{5.8}$$

where maximum $\max_A$ is taken over all the adversaries A with running time $rt2$. Here, q_{O1} represents the number of queries made to Oracle 1. We claim that our scheme is provably secure against an adversary A who tries to derive the session key SK, if $Adv2(rt2, q_O) \le \epsilon$, for any sufficiently smaller $\epsilon > 0$. If by running the trial algorithm $ALGO2_{A,RAS}^{HASH}$, the adversary A has the ability to invert the one-way hash function $h()$, then he or she can deduce the session key SK between the authentication server, IoT application server, and user and win the game. However, inverting the hash function $h()$ is computationally infeasible, i.e., $Adv_A^{HASH}(t) \le \epsilon_1$ (Definition 1), for any sufficiently smaller $\epsilon_1 > 0$. Hence, we have $Adv2(rt2, q_{O1}) \le \epsilon$, since $Adv2(rt, q_{O1})$ depends on the advantage $Adv_A^{HASH}(t)$, for any sufficiently smaller $\epsilon > 0$. This proves that the proposed scheme is secure against an adversary A for deriving the session key SK.

5.6.3 Comparative Analysis

Table 5.8 compares some of the security features of our proposed scheme with other related schemes, i.e., those by Moon et al. [24], Yoon and Yoo [25], and Bae and Kwak [29]. In the Yoon and Yoo [25] scheme and Bae and Kwak [29] scheme, although the schemes operate in a multiserver environment, they do not consider the different security levels for the applications residing on different servers. The Moon et al. [24] scheme does not consider multilevel authentication and is not suitable for the multiserver application environment.

TABLE 5.8 Comparison of security features of our proposed scheme and other related schemes

COMPARISON PARAMETERS	SCHEME			
	MOON ET AL. [24]	YOON & YEE [22]	BAE & KWAK [26]	OUR SCHEME
Provides authentication in multiserver environment	✗	✓	✓	✓
Provides multilevel authentication	✗	✗	✗	✓
Prevents against password guessing attack	✓	✓	✗	✓
Provides user anonymity	✓	✗	✓	✓
Secure server-side password and fingerprint verification	✗	✗	✗	✓

In the Yoon and Yoo [25] scheme, the original identity information of the user in the authenticated key agreement phase is sent to the remote server, and thus, it does not support user anonymity. Moreover, in all three of these schemes, password and biometrics information of the user is verified on the client side, which is vulnerable to client-side verification attacks. Moreover, the Bae and Kwak [29] scheme is susceptible to password guessing attacks in which, if the attacker obtains the smart card, then he or she can enter the guessed password and, if it is correct, would gain access to further authentication process.

5.7 PERFORMANCE ANALYSIS

This section discusses the performance of the proposed scheme by considering the running time of various cryptographic operations involved in it and presents a comparison of the same with three other related schemes, i.e., those by Moon et al. [24], Yoon and Yoo [25], and Bae and Kwak [29]. Table 5.9 summarizes the computational time taken by hashing, EXOR, and symmetric key encryption and decryption operations during all the phases of the model. Table 5.10 shows the comparison of the time complexity of our proposed scheme with other related schemes.

The proposed scheme has fewer hash operations than those of Yoon and Yoo [25] and Bae and Kwak [29]. However, it involves symmetric encryption and decryption to provide user anonymity and untraceability.

TABLE 5.9 Performance analysis of the proposed scheme

PHASE		SYSTEM ENTITIES		
	USER (U_j)	IoT APPLICATION SERVER (IS_j)	AUTHENTICATION SERVER (AS)	TOTAL
Registration	$2t_H$	—	$2t_H + t_E$	$4t_H + t_E$
Security level determination	—	—	—	—
Login	—	—	—	—
Authentication and session key generation	$4t_H + 2t_{EX}$	$3t_H + 4t_{EX}$	$5t_H + 7t_{EX} + t_E + t_D$	$12t_H + 13t_{EX} + t_E + t_D$
Verification	—	—	t_D	t_D
Password change	$4t_H$	—	$2t_E$	$4t_H + 2t_E$
User dismissal	—	—	—	—
Total	$10t_H + 2t_{EX}$	$3t_H + 4t_{EX}$	$7t_H + 7t_{EX} + 4t_E + 2t_D$	$20t_H + 13t_{EX} + 4t_E + 2t_D$

t_H, t_{EX}, t_E / t_D indicate time complexity of executing a hash operation, an EXOR operation, and a symmetric key encryption or decryption operation, respectively.

TABLE 5.10 Comparison of computational cost of proposed and other related schemes

SCHEME	REGISTRATION PHASE	USER LOGIN AND AUTHENTICATION PHASE	PASSWORD CHANGE	TOTAL
Moon et al. [24]	$5t_H + 4t_{EX}$	$7t_H + 5t_{EX}$	$3t_H + 3t_{EX}$	$15t_H + 12t_{EX}$
Yoon & Yoo [25]	$3t_H + t_{EX}$	$16t_H + 2t_{EX}$	$2t_H + 2t_{EX}$	$21t_H + 5t_{EX}$
Bae & Kwak [29]	$5t_H$	$17t_H + 25t_{EX}$	$6t_H$	$28t_H + 25t_{EX}$
Our scheme	$4t_H + t_E$	$12t_H + 13t_{EX} + 3t_E + 2t_D$	$4t_H + 2t_E$	$20t_H + 13t_{EX} + 4t_E + 2t_D$

Users are also free to choose their passwords. The proposed scheme also supports password change phase, which allows users to change the password after verifying the old credentials. In addition, the proposed scheme supports user dismissal phase, which involves revocation of the user's rights in required instances. Moreover, server identity verification is certificate less. In addition, user's credential verification is based on the security policies, which avoids extra computation cost in verifying every authenticator in every application having varying level of security. Moreover, users are not required to provide the values of all the authenticators in different applications. Finally, users can access different applications using a single smart card and the same credentials, which prevents the need to maintain different credentials.

5.8 CONCLUSION AND FUTURE SCOPE

Taking into account the essence of smart cards in IoT applications, we proposed and discussed a multifactor and multiserver remote user authentication scheme based on ECC that uses lightweight cryptographic operations with smaller size keys. The scheme uses flexible multifactor authentication based on smart card, password, biometrics, and OTP. It is suitable for resource-constrained multiserver IoT environments in which a single application can be hosted on multiple servers and the user need not register separately at each server to access the server. Depending on the type of user and the application, the security level for the user is decided. The scheme offers users the ability to freely choose username and password and change their credentials. We also demonstrated an analysis of the security and performance aspects of the scheme to show its effectiveness in relation to other schemes.

Although the results obtained from the experiments are satisfactory and our proposed mechanism is suitable for a variety of applications, we realize that some additional aspects may need to be incorporated in our proposed mechanism. Because this mechanism can be easily upgraded and enhanced, it would be easy to accommodate these extensions. Future work that can be done in relation to the proposed mechanism includes the following:

1. Use of fuzzy extractor to obtain a random string from the user's biometrics provided as input in an error-tolerant fashion. This would increase the security and anonymity of the biometric template used for identifying the users.

2. Inclusion of biometrics update phase through which a user can send the update request for replacing the already stored biometric template with a newer one.
3. Specification of OTP generation process at client side or server side.
4. Inclusion of lost smart card revocation phase, which would involve reissuing a smart card to the user when it is lost, after proper verification.
5. Introduction of machine learning aspects for implementing fraud detection.

By working on these dimensions, this mechanism can be made more powerful against a variety of security attacks and more meaningful for real-time applications.

REFERENCES

1. Gupta, B. B., & Quamara, M. (2018). An identity based access control and mutual authentication framework for distributed cloud computing services in IoT environment using smart cards. *Procedia Computer Science*, *132*, 189–197.
2. Lohachab, A. (2018). Using quantum key distribution and ECC for secure inter-device authentication and communication in IoT infrastructure. Proceedings of the Third International Conference on Internet of Things and Connected Technologies, Jaipur, India, March 26-27, 2018. Retrieved from https://ssrn.com/abstract=3166511
3. Adat, V., & Gupta, B. B. (2018). Security in Internet of Things: Issues, challenges, taxonomy, and architecture. *Telecommunication Systems*, *67*(3), 423–441.
4. Tewari, A., & Gupta, B. B. (2017). A lightweight mutual authentication protocol based on elliptic curve cryptography for IoT devices. *International Journal of Advanced Intelligence Paradigms*, *9*(2-3), 111–121.
5. Tewari, A., & Gupta, B. B. (2017). Cryptanalysis of a novel ultra-lightweight mutual authentication protocol for IoT devices using RFID tags. *The Journal of Supercomputing*, *73*(3), 1085–1102.
6. Stergiou, C., Psannis, K. E., Kim, B. G., & Gupta, B. (2018). Secure integration of IoT and cloud computing. *Future Generation Computer Systems*, *78*, 964–975.
7. Lamport, L. (1981). Password authentication with insecure communication. *Communications of the ACM*, *24*(11), 770–772.
8. Wu, T. C. (1995). Remote login authentication scheme based on a geometric approach. *Computer Communications*, *18*(12), 959–963.
9. Bansal, N., Mahto, D., & Yadav, D. K. (2018). Enhanced RSA key generation modeling using fingerprint biometric. *Helix*, *8*(5), 3922–3926.

10. Jiang, Q., Chen, Z., Li, B., Shen, J., Yang, L., & Ma, J. (2017). Security analysis and improvement of bio-hashing based three-factor authentication scheme for telecare medical information systems. *Journal of Ambient Intelligence and Humanized Computing*, *9*(4), 1061–1073.

11. Soni, P., Ali, R., & Pal, A. K. (2017, July). A two-factor based remote user authentication scheme using ElGamal cryptosystem. In *Proceedings of the ACM Workshop on Internet of Things (IoT) Security: Issues and Innovations* (p. 3). Retrieved from https://www.researchgate.net/publication/321066086_A_Two-factor_based_Remote_User_Authentication_Scheme_using_ElGamal_Cryptosystem

12. Luo, M., Zhang, Y., Khan, M. K., & He, D. (2017). A secure and efficient identity-based mutual authentication scheme with smart card using elliptic curve cryptography. *International Journal of Communication Systems*, *30*(16), e3333.

13. Kumar, R., Amin, R., Karati, A., & Biswas, G. P. (2016). Secure remote login scheme with password and smart card update facilities. In S. Das, T. Pal, S. Kar, S. Satapathy, & J. Mandal (Eds.), *Proceedings of the 4th International Conference on Frontiers in Intelligent Computing: Theory and Applications (FICTA) 2015. Advances in Intelligent Systems and Computing* (vol. 404, pp. 26–33). New Delhi, India: Springer.

14. Limbasiya, T., & Doshi, N. (2017). An analytical study of biometric based remote user authentication schemes using smart cards. *Computers & Electrical Engineering*, *59*, 305–321.

15. Yang, W. H., & Shieh, S. P. (1999). Password authentication schemes with smart cards. *Computers & Security*, *18*(8), 727–733.

16. Hwang, M. S., & Li, L. H. (2000). A new remote user authentication scheme using smart cards. *IEEE Transactions on Consumer Electronics*, *46*(1), 28–30.

17. Shen, J. J., Lin, C. W., & Hwang, M. S. (2003). A modified remote user authentication scheme using smart cards. *IEEE Transactions on Consumer Electronics*, *49*(2), 414–416.

18. Ku, W. C., & Chen, S. M. (2004). Weaknesses and improvements of an efficient password based remote user authentication scheme using smart cards. *IEEE Transactions on Consumer Electronics*, *50*(1), 204–207.

19. Li, C. T., & Hwang, M. S. (2010). An efficient biometrics-based remote user authentication scheme using smart cards. *Journal of Network and Computer Applications*, *33*(1), 1–5.

20. Li, X., Niu, J. W., Ma, J., Wang, W. D., & Liu, C. L. (2011). Cryptanalysis and improvement of a biometrics-based remote user authentication scheme using smart cards. *Journal of Network and Computer Applications*, *34*(1), 73–79.

21. Das, A. K. (2011). Analysis and improvement on an efficient biometric-based remote user authentication scheme using smart cards. *IET Information Security*, *5*(3), 145–151.

22. An, Y. (2012). Security analysis and enhancements of an effective biometric-based remote user authentication scheme using smart cards. *Journal of Biomedicine and Biotechnology*, 2012, 519723. Retrieved from https://www.hindawi.com/journals/bmri/2012/519723/

23. Mutlugun, M., & Sogukpinar, I. (2009, June). Multi-level authentication scheme utilizing smart cards and biometrics. In *Emerging Security Information, Systems and Technologies, 2009. SECURWARE'09. Third International Conference on* (pp. 93–98). New York, NY: IEEE.

24. Moon, J., Lee, D., Jung, J., & Won, D. (2017). Improvement of efficient and secure smart card based password authentication scheme. *IJ Network Security*, *19*(6), 1053–1061.
25. Yoon, E. J., & Yoo, K. Y. (2013). Robust biometrics-based multi-server authentication with key agreement scheme for smart cards on elliptic curve cryptosystem. *The Journal of Supercomputing*, *63*(1), 235–255.
26. Chuang, M. C., & Chen, M. C. (2014). An anonymous multi-server authenticated key agreement scheme based on trust computing using smart cards and biometrics. *Expert Systems with Applications*, *41*(4), 1411–1418.
27. Mishra, D., Das, A. K., & Mukhopadhyay, S. (2014). A secure user anonymity-preserving biometric-based multi-server authenticated key agreement scheme using smart cards. *Expert Systems with Applications*, *41*(18), 8129–8143.
28. He, D., & Wang, D. (2015). Robust biometrics-based authentication scheme for multiserver environment. *IEEE Systems Journal*, *9*(3), 816–823.
29. Bae, W. I., & Kwak, J. (2017). Smart card-based secure authentication protocol in multi-server IoT environment. *Multimedia Tools and Applications*, *1–19*. Retrieved from https://link.springer.com/article/10.1007/s11042-017-5548-2
30. Miller, V. S. (1985, August). Use of elliptic curves in cryptography. In *Conference on the Theory and Application of Cryptographic Techniques* (pp. 417–426). Berlin, Germany: Springer.
31. Koblitz, N. (1987). Elliptic curve cryptosystems. *Mathematics of Computation*, *48*(177), 203–209.
32. Ciet, M., Joye, M., Lauter, K., & Montgomery, P. L. (2006). Trading inversions for multiplications in elliptic curve cryptography. *Designs, Codes and Cryptography*, *39*(2), 189–206.
33. Kumari, S., Chaudhry, S. A., Wu, F., Li, X., Farash, M. S., & Khan, M. K. (2017). An improved smart card based authentication scheme for session initiation protocol. *Peer-to-Peer Networking and Applications*, *10*(1), 92–105.
34. Dolev, D., & Yao, A. (1983). On the security of public key protocols. *IEEE Transactions on Information Theory*, *29*(2), 198–208.
35. Kocher, P., Jaffe, J., Jun, B., & Rohatgi, P. (2011). Introduction to differential power analysis. *Journal of Cryptographic Engineering*, *1*(1), 5–27.
36. The AVISPA Project. (n.d.). Home page. Retrieved from http://www.avispa-project.org
37. NIST-CSRC. (2019). Access Control Policy Testing. Retrieved from https://csrc.nist.gov/Projects/Access-Control-Policy-Tool
38. Chuang, Y. H., & Tseng, Y. M. (2010). An efficient dynamic group key agreement protocol for imbalanced wireless networks. *International Journal of Network Management*, *20*(4), 167–180.
39. Odelu, V., Das, A. K., & Goswami, A. (2016). A secure and efficient time-bound hierarchical access control scheme for secure broadcasting. *International Journal of Ad Hoc and Ubiquitous Computing*, *22*(4), 236–248.

Smart Card Communication Standards, Applications, and Development Tools

6

6.1 INTRODUCTION

Rapid evolution and advancement of smart card technology in the past couple of years have spurred the development of high-quality standards that can be used to expand smart card–based applications. Although the standard-making process is complex, various domestic and international organizations are working in collaboration to bring about better results. Moreover, a clear understanding of how smart cards are being used in various application areas is required, along with an understanding of the tools that are used for their development and maintenance. In this chapter, we discuss all three aspects of smart card technology. In the next section, we highlight various communication standards for smart card–based systems and applications.

6.2 COMMUNICATION STANDARDS

Communication standards are a set of rules that are developed by industries for defining and governing the function of the systems and devices that are a part of digital communication and are involved in exchange of messages. These formulate the structure, semantics, and overall synchronization among the communicating entities and can be executed at hardware level, software level, or both. For effective implementation of digital systems, development of high-quality standards is necessary.

Different communication standards have been defined by various standard-making bodies across the globe for smart card–based systems and applications, taking into account the nature of applications, types of cards, and other such factors. These standards and standard-making bodies are summarized in Table 6.1 and are discussed in brief as follows:

1. **International Standards Organization (ISO)/International Eletrotechnical Commission (IEC) Standards**—ISO is a global standard-making body that facilitates the standard creation process, which is open to all parties. Primary ISO/IEC standards for smart cards include ISO/IEC 7816 (which comprises 14 different parts), ISO/IEC 14443, ISO/IEC 15693, and ISO/IEC 7501 [1].
2. **Federal Information Processing Standards (FIPS)**—These standards are defined by the Computer Security Division of the National Institute of Standards and Technology (NIST) for protecting federal computing and telecommunication systems [2].
3. **American National Standards Institute (ANSI)**—ANSI recommends standards specific to the needs of the United States and monitors and controls the activities associated with the standard-making process [3].
4. **G-8 Health Standards**—G-8 countries collaborate in work on defining the standard format for storing data on healthcare cards, file formats, and digital certificate usage [4].
5. **Europay, MasterCard, Visa (EMV) Standards**—EMV is a global standard for financial transactions involving chip-based smart cards and payment terminals (automated teller machines [ATM] and point-of-sale [PoS] terminals). Initially, the EMV standard started as a terminal specification. However, later on, it evolved to contain four books [5].
6. **Biometric Standards**—Because newer smart card–based system implementations use biometrics, various biometric standards have

TABLE 6.1   Smart card communication standards

STANDARD		DESCRIPTION
ISO/IEC 7816	1–3	Contact smart cards aspects (physical characteristics), electrical characteristics, electronic signals, communication protocols
	4–6, 8–9, 11, 13, 15	Contact and contactless smart cards logical structure (data and file elements), commands for interfacing, cryptographic services, application identification, management and naming, and biometric verification
	7	Secure relational database approach based on Structured Card Query Language (SCQL) interfaces
	10	Memory cards (power signals, signal structure)
ISO/IEC 14443		Interfaces (electrical interface, radiofrequency [RF]) for close proximity contactless smart cards, anticollision protocols, communication protocols
ISO/IEC 15693		Vicinity card's physical characteristic, interface (RF power and signal), transmission protocol, anticollision protocol
ISO/IEC 7501		Machine-readable travel documents
FIPS 140 (1-3)		Security requirements for design and execution of the cryptographic module
FIPS 201		Physical and logical access cards with contact and contactless interfaces, all aspects of multifunction cards
FIPS 186-2		Generation and verification of digital signatures
ANSI X9.31-1998		Rivest-Shamir-Adleman (RSA) signature algorithm
ANSI X9.62-1998		ECDSA signature algorithm
FIPS 197		Advanced Encryption Standard (AES)
FIPS 140		Secure design and execution of cryptographic module
ANSI		Recommendation for standards
G-8 Health Standards		Storage, file formats, and digital certificates for health cards
EMV Standards	Book 1	Application Independent Integrated Circuit Card (ICC) to Terminal Interface Requirements
	Book 2	Security and Key Management
	Book 3	Application Specification
	Book 4	Cardholder, Attendant, and Acquirer Interface Requirements

(Continued)

TABLE 6.1 *(Continued)* Smart card communication standards

STANDARD		DESCRIPTION
Biometric Standards	ANSI-INCITS 358-2002	BioAPI Specification (ISO/IEC 19784-1)
	ANSI-INCITS 398	Common Biometric Exchange Formats Framework (CBEFF) (ISO/IEC 19785-1)
	ANSI-INCITS	Biometric Data Format Interchange Standards
	ANSI-INCITS 377-2004	Finger Pattern–Based Interchange Format
	ANSI-INCITS 378-2004	Finger Minutiae Format for Data Interchange
	ANSI-INCITS 379-2004	Iris-Interchange Format
	ANSI-INCITS 381-2004	Finger Image–Based Interchange Format
	ANSI-INCITS 381-2004	Face Recognition Format for Data Interchange
	ANSI-INCITS 385-2004	Face Recognition Format for Data Interchange
	ANSI-INCITS 395-2005	Signature/Sign Image–Based Interchange Format
	ANSI-INCITS 396-2004	Hand Geometry Interchange Format
	ISO/IEC 19794	Series on Biometric Data Interchange Formats (Part 1 – the framework; Part 2 – defines the finger minutiae data; Part 3 – defines finger pattern spectral data; Part 4 – defines the finger image data; Part 5 – defines the face image data; Part 6 – defines the iris image data; Part 7 – defines the signature/sign time series data; Part 8 – defines the finger pattern skeletal data; Part 8 – defines the vascular image data)
PC/SC Workgroup Specifications		Microprocessor card aspects including cryptographic functionality, secure storage, and programming and application interface
GP Standards		Secure components for smart cards
IATA		Aspects for smart cards in transport industry
GSM		Subscriber Identity Module (SIM) cards

also been defined to improve the overall security of the corresponding applications [1].

7. **Personal Computer/Smart Card (PC/SC) Workgroup Specifications**—The PC/SC Workgroup was formed by collaboration of some of the leading vendors across the globe, including Bull CP8, Schlumberger Electronic Transactions, Microsoft, Hewlett-Packard (HP), and so forth, in 1996. It defines open and platform-independent specification for smart cards in integration with personal computers (microprocessor cards), including aspects such as cryptographic functionality, secure storage, and programming and application interface [2].

8. **GlobalPlatform (GP)**—GP is a nonprofit international association that standardizes and certifies a secure hardware and firmware combination, which is also known as a secure component. It helps in establishing collaboration among device manufacturers and service providers for defining the appropriate level of security required to protect the digital systems and devices against security threats [2].

9. **International Airline and Transportation Association (IATA)**—The IATA defines standards for the transportation and airline industry. It develops interoperability standards for ticketless travel using smart cards [6].

10. **Global System for Mobile Communication (GSM) Standards**—These include various telecommunication standards, including standards for subscriber identity module (SIM) cards that are embedded with information required to authenticate GSM-compliant mobile phones [7]. The European Telecommunication Standards Institute manages the GSM standards.

6.3 APPLICATION AREAS

In this section, we discuss the various application areas of smart cards.

1. **Financial applications**—To facilitate customers and business organizations with value-added services at lower overall cost for each transaction, smart cards are being widely used by financial companies across the world. Typical financial services that use smart cards include cash stores, loyalty programs, and other marketing programs. Debit cards involve deduction of the amount from the card holder's account, whereas credit cards involve borrowing

money from the card-issuing organization. Contactless payment services are becoming popular as they surpass the need of physical contact between the payment devices and the PoS terminals. Samsung Pay, Apple Pay, and Google Pay are examples of contactless payment services [8–10]. Although card fraud is an important concern in these applications, which keeps growing with increasing card usage, organizations are taking appropriate measures for their mass adoption [11].

2. **Telecommunication applications**—Smart cards are being extensively used in telecommunications in the form of prepaid telephone cards, subscriber identity module (SIM) cards, and Universal Integrated Circuit Cards (UICC), which uniquely identify every subscriber and ensure authentication to provide network access. Prepaid telephone cards are memory cards with stored value associated with the amount for accessing the telephonic services. This amount is deducted after every transaction made by the card holder. Conversely, SIM cards are microcontroller-based smart cards that signify subscribers over the network and facilitate access to services (including data, voice, and videos) and global roaming while traveling in remote locations. SIM cards are also used to store contact information of other people and messages. UICCs are an optimized form of SIM technology that comply with the latest wireless sensor network (WSN) standards and provide enhanced capabilities, better support for IP addressing, and multiple applications [12].

3. **Access control applications**—Smart cards typically contain digital signatures belonging to individuals, which provides a special mechanism to ensure secure and legitimate access to corporation networks and network resources and to avoid the risks of unauthorized entities breaking into the system. In the United States, the Department of Defense issues smart cards to military personnel and other employees to ensure authorized physical and logical access to the networks and systems [13].

4. **Broadcasting applications**—Smart cards are more often used in the form of direct-to-home (DTH) cards for providing authorized access to the remote services and information coming from satellites for which the cryptographic operations are performed on the card itself [14].

5. **Retail and E-commerce applications**—Smart cards are fundamental building blocks of e-commerce applications because they facilitate low-cost transactions and are used for storing account- and transaction-specific information of the customers. They also support customization of services. For example, it has become possible

to buy tailored services on the World Wide Web [15]. Loyalty cards are issued by retailers that store points or credit for providing discounts and other benefits in future transactions.

6. **Government applications**—Governments issue smart cards to individuals that are used to identify the card holders using the identifying information stored on them, including name, date of birth, location, and so on. An example of this is the Aadhar card in India [16].

7. **Healthcare applications**—Medical organizations across the world are making use of smart cards to support diverse features in healthcare applications. These cards not only provide security and privacy to the patient-specific information, but also act as a portable solution to carrying medical records in compliance with government regulations and guidelines [17].

8. **Transportation applications**—Millions of smart cards are currently in use in transit and fee payment applications. Stored value prepaid cards are used for electronic ticketing by transit agencies across the globe. Contactless cards are used for automatic fare collection at toll stations and parking areas. User travel records can also be stored in the smart cards, and these data can later be mined and analyzed for understanding the mobility patterns of the users for facilitating better services and urban management [18].

6.4 OPEN SOURCE TOOLS

In this section, we discuss some of the open-source tools for designing, creating, and validating smart card–based systems and applications. These are summarized in Table 6.2 and are discussed in detail in the following subsections.

6.4.1 Development Tools

Some of the commonly used open-source development tools for smart card technology are as follows:

1. **Open Smart Card Development Platform (OpenSCDP) [19]**—OpenSCDP comprises various Java- and JavaScript-based tools that are used for developing, installing, and screening smart card–based applications. It utilizes capabilities of various technologies,

TABLE 6.2 Open-source tools for smart card technology

TOOL CATEGORY	TOOL EXAMPLE
Development tools	Open Smart Card Development Platform (OpenSCDP) (Smart Card Shell 3, Smart Card Scripting Environment for Eclipse [SSE4E], Scripting Server); Java Card Development Kit; SkyCard; Cardpeek
Middleware libraries	Java Card Pro; OpenSC; SIM Application Toolkit
Key stores	GNU Privacy Guard (GnuPG); EMV Key Manager
Certificate authority software	Enterprise Java Beans Certificate Authority (EJBCA); Dogtag Certificate System
Testing tools	Secunet Global Tester; SmartLogic Tool

such as Global Platform Scripting, Messaging, and Profiling, for providing speedy and flexible development. Contact and contactless smart card–based access using Application Protocol Data Unit (APDU) is enabled through OpenCard Framework (OCF), which is a Java-based middleware. Drivers are typically included for PC/SC, smart cards based on ISO 7816-4, and Card Terminal-Application Programming Interface (CT-API) card readers. Full support for cryptographic algorithms used by smart cards is also provided. The tools are discussed as follows:

1.1 *Smart Card Shell 3*—This is a JavaScript-based scripting and interactive development Java-based tool that allows easy accessibility to the smart cards on file system and APDU level. It is used for developing and testing smart card–based applications, particularly the ones that are integrated with public key infrastructure (PKI).

1.2 *Smart Card Scripting Environment for Eclipse (SSE4E)*—This is an Eclipse plug-in that facilitates an interactive scripting platform for developing and testing smart card–based applications. It supports cards compliant with ISO 7816-4. It also uses JavaScript as command and scripting language.

1.3 *Scripting Server*—This is a server equivalent of Smart Card Shell and provides an execution environment for smart card–based applications that are written in JavaScript. It permits prototyping and testing of cryptographic services and corresponding applications. It is typically deployed in a servlet container and uses JavaScript as scripting language.

2. **Java Card Development Kit [20]**—This provides a set of tools and a stand-alone environment for designing and implementing Java Card technology and for the development of applets based on the

Java Card API specification. It enables conversion and verification of the Java Card applications and provides a simulation environment for testing and debugging.

3. **SkyCard [21]**—This is an open-source graphical tool for handling synchronous memory-based smart cards.

4. **Cardpeek [22]**—This is an open-source tool for reading the content of the smart cards and uses GTK Graphical User Interface (GUI) for representing the same in a tree view. It is extensible with LUA scripting language.

6.4.2 Middleware Libraries

Middleware libraries for smart card–based application development are discussed as follows:

1. **Java Card Pro [23]**—This is an open-source component library for the development, enhancement, loading, and management of secure Java Card applets within a small time frame.

2. **OpenSC [24]**—This comprises a set of libraries and software tools for smart cards and emphasizes the cryptographic capabilities of smart cards. It enables the utilization of smart cards in a variety of applications, including digital signatures, encryption, and validation. It implements PKCS #11 API and PKCS #15 standards.

3. **SIM Application Toolkit [25]**—This is a set of commands that are used to define the interaction of smart cards with the external environment, along with the extension of communication protocols to the SIM card and handset device.

6.4.3 Key Stores

Key stores for smart card technology are discussed as follows:

1. **GNU Privacy Guard (GnuPG) [26]**—This is a command line tool and an open-source execution of the OpenPGP standard defined by RFC4880. It enables encryption and signature over the data and ongoing communication by using a versatile key administration system and access modules for open key catalogs. It also supports Secure Shell (SSH) and S/MIME.

2. **EMV Key Manager [27]**—This is used to manage a diverse set of cryptographic keys among authorized parties for various EMV smart card–based applications.

6.4.4 Certificate Authority Software

Certificate authority software programs for smart card technology are discussed as follows:

1. **Enterprise Java Beans Certificate Authority (EJBCA) [28]**— This is a Java-based PKI certificate authority software that can be used on its own or integrated with other applications.
2. **Dogtag Certificate System [29]**—This is an open-source enterprise certificate authority that supports and manages all the phases of the certificate life cycle, including certificate issuance, profiling, revocation, and retrieval, in smart card–based applications.

6.4.5 Testing Tools

Testing tools for smart card technology are discussed as follows:

1. **Secunet Global Tester [30]**—This is an open-source testing tool for smart card protocols. It enables flexible and quick customization of applications and additional features by customers. Other features include comprehensive failure analysis, support, quick implementation of test specifications, and so forth.
2. **SmartLogic Tool [31]**—This is a tool for performing research on smart card technology that enables complete control over the transmission channel for broadcasting, card emulation, and a wide range of security attacks, including man-in-the-middle (MITM), eavesdropping, and so forth.

6.5 CONCLUSION

In this chapter, we discussed various communication standards and application areas of smart cards along with various open-source tools that are available for designing, developing, and testing of smart card–based systems and applications.

In the next chapter, we will discuss the role of blockchain and quantum computing in smart card technology to showcase the future aspects of the technology in the presence of advanced innovations.

REFERENCES

1. QCard: The Lab Authority. (n.d.). Smart card standards. Retrieved from https://www.q-card.com/about-us/smart-card-standards/page.aspx?id=1461
2. Secure Technology Alliance. (2019). Smart card standards and specifications. Retrieved from https://www.securetechalliance.org/smart-cards-intro-standards/#personal-computersmart-card-workgroup-open-specifications
3. ANSI. (2006). Overarching smart card standard earns ISO and IEC recognition. Retrieved from https://www.ansi.org/news_publications/news_story?menuid=7&articleid=43f2deed-eb91-42c5-ab1c-0563d5eb9778
4. STS. (2018). G8, on-board. Retrieved from https://www.stspayments.com/snippets/g8-on-board
5. Smart Card Basics. (2010). Smart card standards. Retrieved from http://www.smartcardbasics.com/smart-card-standards.html
6. Atkins, W. (Ed.). (2012). *The smart card report*. New York, NY: Elsevier.
7. Chudo, M. (2011). The communication protocol for GSM card. Retrieved from https://is.muni.cz/th/324546/fi_b/text.pdf
8. Samsung. (n.d.). Samsung Pay. Retrieved from https://www.samsung.com/in/samsung-pay/
9. Apple. (n.d.). Apple Pay. Retrieved from https://www.apple.com/apple-pay/
10. Google. (n.d.). GPay. Retrieved from https://pay.google.com/intl/en_in/about/
11. Markantonakis, K., & Main, D. (2017). Smart cards for Banking and Finance. In *Smart cards, tokens, security and applications* (pp. 129–153). Cham, Switzerland: Springer.
12. Becker, T., Nichols, P. W., Calamusa, M., Horton, M., & Osterwise, R. (2018). U.S. Patent Application No. 15/271,135. Washington, DC: U.S. Patent and Trademark Office.
13. Finkenzeller, K. (2010). *RFID handbook: Fundamentals and applications in contactless smart cards, radio frequency identification and near-field communication*. New York, NY: John Wiley & Sons.
14. Gupta, B. B., & Quamara, M. (2018, October). A dynamic security policies generation model for access control in smart card based applications. In *International Symposium on Cyberspace Safety and Security* (pp. 132–143). Cham, Switzerland: Springer.
15. Elecetronic Commerce Payment System. (n.d.). Smart cards. Retrieved from https://electroniccommercepaymentsystem.weebly.com/3-smart-cards.html
16. Ghangare, A., & Ranade, A. (2018). Aadhar card: Perspectives on privacy. Retrieved from www.preprints.org
17. Stafford, N. (2015). Germany is set to introduce e-health cards by 2018. *BMJ, 350*, h2991.
18. Ma, X., Wu, Y. J., Wang, Y., Chen, F., & Liu, J. (2013). Mining smart card data for transit riders' travel patterns. *Transportation Research Part C: Emerging Technologies, 36*, 1–12.
19. Open Smart Card Development Platform. (n.d.). Retrieved from https://www.openscdp.org

20. Oracle. (n.d.). Retrieved from https://www.oracle.com/technetwork/java/embed-ded/javacard/downloads/javacard-sdk-2043229.html
21. Source Forge. (n.d.). Retrieved from https://sourceforge.net/projects/skycard/
22. Cardpeek. (n.d.). Retrieved from http://pannetrat.com/Cardpeek/
23. JavaCard Pro. (n.d.). Retrieved from https://javacard.pro
24. Github. (n.d.). Retrieved from https://github.com/OpenSC/OpenSC/wiki
25. Gemalto. (n.d.). Retrieved from https://www.gemalto.com/companyinfo/digital-security/techno/stk
26. GnuPG. (n.d.). Retrieved from https://www.gnupg.org
27. Rambus. (n.d.). Retrieved from https://www.rambus.com/security/payments/mobile-payments/emv-smart-card-management/
28. EJBCA PKI by PrimeKey. (n.d.). Retrieved from https://www.ejbca.org
29. Dogtag. (n.d.). Retrieved from https://www.dogtagpki.org/wiki/PKI_Main_Page
30. Secunet. (n.d.). Retrieved from https://globaltester.secunet.com
31. de Koning Gans, G., & De Ruiter, J. (2012, April). The SmartLogic tool: Analysing and testing smart card protocols. In *2012 IEEE Fifth International Conference on Software Testing, Verification and Validation* (pp. 864–871). IEEE.

Blockchain Integration and Quantum Smart Cards

7

7.1 INTRODUCTION

Smart cards can be described as microcomputers embedded over the card that are capable of storing crucial information associated with the card holder and that incorporate various data reading and writing technologies. Smart cards are easy to use and affordable for a wide range of applications. Blockchain can be considered a revolutionary concept that is capable of fulfilling the strict security requirements to help business organizations in developing secure applications. Blockchain can also be considered as a perfect match for smart card technology for effective management of cryptographic data.

In real-time smart card–based applications, identity theft and card fraud are deliberate threats that are a huge concern for industries and consumers. To safeguard the crucial financial data and personal identifying information from such criminal activities, new innovations are being developed. The idea of quantum computing is expected to provide an enhanced level of security in applications involving complex cryptographic operations and, hence, can be integrated with smart card technology.

In the next section, we discuss in detail the role of blockchain technology in securing smart card–based applications.

7.2 BLOCKCHAIN TECHNOLOGY

In this section, we discuss the blockchain technology and its role in securing smart card–based applications.

7.2.1 What Is Blockchain Technology?

Blockchain is an undeniably insightful invention that allows digital information to be distributed instead of copied and, thus, has created a new backbone for today's Internet. This technology was originally devised to be used in the form of digital currency, such as Bitcoin, by Satoshi Nakamoto in 2008, for which it was implemented in 2009. However, people in the technological community are finding many other effective uses of the technology.

Blockchain empowers a decentralized data storage service in which a tamper-resistant ledger is composed of blocks that are chained in sequential fashion [1]. It uses cryptographic aspects for recording and securing transactional events. The fundamental unit of blockchain is transaction, which when produced, is communicated to the whole network. These transactions are accompanied by signatures that are used for validation on receipt by the network nodes. After successful verification, the transactions are mined into blocks that are cryptographically secured. These nodes are called block miners and are required to solve a consensus problem in a distributed fashion for creating the block. Those miners that are able to solve the problem, and communicate the new blocks corresponding to them to all the nodes in the network. On receipt of the new block, the miners that have not yet been able to solve the problem append the new block in their own blockchain maintained by them locally. The new block contains a connection or link to the previous block in the chain through the use of cryptographic mechanisms. Once all the transactions that are enclosed in the block are checked, the block is considered to solve and provide the substantial answer for the consensus problem. All the miners are able to synchronize their chains periodically. Specific terms are defined for ensuring ledger consistency, which is shared across all the nodes in the network.

7.2.2 Smart Cards and Blockchain

Blockchain integrated with smart cards is capable of producing an efficient solution that would not only support businesses and industries to earn more revenue, but also ensure retention of more customers. Smart card is a secure, portable, and easy-to-use platform and provides the capability of storing private keys that can be used for performing transactions involving cryptocurrencies. Blockchain technology can be used in diverse financial and non-financial smart card–based applications, as discussed below:

1. **Identity management and access control**—Blockchain technology provides improved techniques, such as digitization of personal documents, for ensuring effective identification and verification that can be used in smart card–based online transactions.

   Rouhani et al. [2] proposed a management system for physical access control using permissioned blockchain. The authors used Hyperledger Fabric and Hyperledger Composer for implementing secured access to physical locations. A transaction log, which contains the historical records of the already submitted transactions, is provided by the system for querying, which is accessible to the legitimate users only. Moreover, transaction history is secured because it is tamper-proof.

2. **Finance**—Blockchain can be integrated with the contactless payment card systems to avail the benefits of both physical and digital systems.

   Godfrey-Welch et al. [3] discussed the role of blockchain technology in payment card systems, along with the constraints, risks, and ethical aspects associated with this use.

3. **Generation and protection of cryptographic keys of the users**—Smart cards involve generation of cryptographic keys at lower power consumption and with high level of security due to the use of a hardware-based secure element, which protects the keys from advanced security attacks. This limits the interaction to a set of fewer commands and corresponding responses.

4. **Secure access to cryptographic keys**—Blockchain integrated with smart cards allows the use of multiple form factors, which ensures user-controlled and portable access to the cryptographic keys involved in various transactions.

5. **Standardized implementation environment**—Blockchain integrated with smart card technology implements security platforms and evaluations based on standards and certificate-based programs.

7.3 QUANTUM SMART CARDS

In this section, we discuss the concept of quantum computing and its role in smart card technology.

7.3.1 What Is Quantum Computing?

Advancements in the fields of computer science, mathematics, and material science over the past five decades have turned the concept of quantum computing into reality. It is a discipline that focuses on the development of computing systems that are based on the quantum theory principles. By adopting the laws of quantum physics, quantum computers would obtain extensive processing capabilities through the ability to stay in multiple states and solve all possible permutations of problems in parallel. These systems are expected to take modern computing far beyond the current realm. Cloud technology can be used to access quantum computers in real time, and researchers are engaged in conducting research on them for solving new problems. Quantum computing has the potential to revolutionize various disciplines, including healthcare, complex system optimization, machine learning, and artificial intelligence.

The concept of quantum computing was investigated in the early 20th century, and it arose as a separate discipline between 1970s and 1980s [4]. In the 1990s, high-speed algorithms for quantum computers were developed, along with other discoveries that led to an increasing interest in the field with fundamental understanding. With the advent of transmon qubit, significant progress can be seen in the development of real-time systems and experiments associated with them [5]. Organizations and research centers, including IBM, MIT, and Oxford University, are conducting research in this area.

In a quantum computer, elementary particles, such as photons or electrons, can be used, and their polarization represents bits among 0 and 1. These particles are known as quantum bits or qubits, and the behavior of these particles is fundamental to quantum computing. Some of the key aspects associated with quantum theory are superposition and entangled qubits. Superposition is a phenomenon in which qubit is in both state 0 and 1 simultaneously. Unlike conventional bits that carry the value either 0 or 1 at a time, operations performed on qubits can provide results for both of the inputs at the same time. This available parallelism can become huge when multiple qubits are arranged in a register because the overall parallelism is increased by a factor of 2. The concept of entanglement states that when an operation is performed on one of the elements of the entangled pair, it will have an impact on the other one automatically. More state combinations ensure more storage space, and thus, when conventional computers run out of space while solving problems, quantum computers can be seen as a possible alternative.

7.3.2 Quantum Smart Cards

Quantum computing is believed to have the potential to break into the systems based on current cryptographic algorithms. Thus, it is necessary to prepare these systems for future innovations, such as quantum computing. Standard-making bodies are also working on the development and release of single or multiple post-quantum cryptography–based algorithms to avoid quantum hacking [6].

Smart card–based identification systems have the following fundamental issues:

1. An unknown terminal point can be manipulated to memorize the unique information by the user, such as personal identification numbers (PIN) in ATM machines.
2. An eavesdropper can memorize the PIN along with the unknown point of terminal.
3. Non-invasive attacks can lead to damage to the smart card–based silicon chip without the card coming in contact with the teller machine.

Because all carriers of the information in conventional smart card–based systems are physical and are exposed to cloning and copying, card identifying information can be enclosed by the manipulation of the physical properties of the card, which enables an eavesdropper to measure the key related information in a precise fashion. Such problems can be resolved by quantum computing. An eavesdropper in quantum channels can be easily detected.

The first effective implementation of smart cards based on post-quantum cryptography at the commercial level was demonstrated by a German semiconductor manufacturer, Infineon Technologies [7]. Smart card contactless microcontroller chips were used for the implementation of post-quantum cryptography, which demanded the re-engineering of the chip to enhance the memory and data transfer capabilities for the execution of highly computation-intensive and complex algorithms. To establish a secure encrypted communication channel between the two communicating parties, key exchange schemes were used. Post-quantum cryptography–based cards have found their use in various security-intensive applications, including passports.

Scientists from Los Alamos National laboratory (LANL) also developed a quantum smart card, QKarD, which uses the concept of quantum computing instead of mathematical aspects for encrypting information [8]. It involves the use of polarized single photons for secret key generation, which is shared among communicating parties for data encryption and ensures forward security. QKarD is periodically inserted by the users into the base station for authentication, which requires both a fingerprint and PIN. Optical fibers are used for communicating with the trusted authority (TA) and for automatically uploading the cryptographic-quality secret random numbers that are stored on the device's memory for the purpose of authentication.

In one study [9], a smart card application based on quantum cryptography involving quantum transmission of photons and utilization of quantum key distribution for identification systems was published. In another publication [10], a quantum cryptography–based identification solution was proposed for smart card–based applications. It involves the projection on an already selected polarization basis of the photon from the Einstein-Podolsky-Rosen (EPR) pair of polarized photons over the card itself. The system is based on the concept of quantum entanglement of two photons. The card is supposed to have an opto-electronic device that is activated by typing the PIN directly on the card, which avoids sending the PIN to the teller machine. Non-local projection of the state of one of the members of the pair of entangled photons protects information against eavesdroppers. Moreover, the power source is built onto the card itself (photocell).

Quantum cryptography–based key distribution can be used to secure smart card–based communications using quantum mechanics. In such a scenario, no computational assumptions are to be involved, and it would include the use of fiber-optic cables for transmission. Post-quantum cryptography can be deployed without the use of quantum computers and is believed to ensure better security against conventional and quantum computing attacks. The aim of post-quantum cryptography is to replace the already existing asymmetric algorithms, such as the Rivest-Shamir-Adleman (RSA) Algorithm and elliptic curve cryptography (ECC).

7.4 CONCLUSION

In this chapter, we discussed the role of blockchain technology and quantum computing when designing secure smart card–based systems and applications.

REFERENCES

1. Wang, X., Zha, X., Ni, W., Liu, R. P., Guo, Y. J., Niu, X., & Zheng, K. (2019). Survey on blockchain for Internet of Things. *Computer Communications, 136*. Retrieved from https://www.researchgate.net/publication/330351295_Survey_on_Blockchain_for_Internet_of_Things
2. Rouhani, S., Pourheidari, V., & Deters, R. (2019). Physical access control management system based on permissioned blockchain. *arXiv preprint arXiv:1901.09873*. Retrieved from https://arxiv.org/abs/1901.09873

3. Godfrey-Welch, D., Lagrois, R., Law, J., & Anderwald, R. S. (2018). Blockchain in payment card systems. *SMU Data Science Review*, *1*(1), 3.
4. IBM Q. (n.d.). What is quantum computing. Retrieved from https://www. research.ibm.com/ibm-q/learn/what-is-quantum-computing/
5. Burnett, J., Bengtsson, A., Scigliuzzo, M., Niepce, D., Kudra, M., Delsing, P., & Bylander, J. (2019). Decoherence benchmarking of superconducting qubits. *arXiv preprint arXiv:1901.04417*. Retrieved from https://arxiv.org/abs/1901.04417
6. NIS Summer School. (2018). ENISA-FORTH SUMMER SCHOOL on Network & Information Security. Retrieved from https://nis-summer-school.enisa.europa. eu/2018/cources/monday/20180924_PQC_Poeppelmann_NIS.pdf
7. SecureIDNews. (2017). Post-quantum cryptography on smart cards demonstrated by Infineon. Retrieved from https://www.secureidnews.com/news-item/post-quantum-cryptography-on-smart-cards-demonstrated-by-infineon/
8. Los Alamos National Laboratory. (n.d.). QKarD Quantum Smart Card. Retrieved from https://www.lanl.gov/projects/feynman-center/_assets/pdf/qkard.pdf
9. Hruby, J. (1995, July). Smart-card with Interferometric quantum cryptography device. In *International Conference on Cryptography: Policy and Algorithms* (pp. 282–289). Berlin, Germany: Springer.
10. Hrubý, J. (2001). New physical attacks and security of smart-card. *Biometric System for Generating of Nontransferable Private Keys*. Retrieved from http://spi.unob.cz/papers/2001/2001-15.pdf

Index